TWO GOO READING THIS GUIDE

First Reason: Your selection interviews are producing an unacceptable number of marginal or poor performers and *you want to improve your selection interviewing practices* to consistently select good performers.

Second Reason: *You need to improve your knowledge about how to plan and conduct a structured, behavioral interview - the best type of interview to use.*

Not sure about the above reasons? Assess yourself by reading the next section and completing the quiz that follows it.

ASSESSING YOUR CURRENT SELECTION INTERVIEWING PRACTICES

The following statements describe *effective selection interviewing practices*. How do your current practices compare?

- Selection criteria for the vacant position are identified and defined in advance of the interview.
- The identified selection criteria correlate with successful position performance. In other words, they are all bona fide occupational requirements/qualifications.
- All interview questions focus on the success selection criteria.
- A large majority of the interview questions are behavioral. Example: Tell us about a time in the last six months when you suggested an improvement idea to your supervisor.
- Almost all of the interview questions are prepared in advance.
- The candidate's application information is read before the interview and the behavioral questions are tailored to fit the information, when possible.

- Hypothetical or situational questions are not used. Examples: What would you do if...? If you were in the situation of ..., what would you do?
- Leading questions are avoided. Example: Are you a team player?
- No illegal/unacceptable questions are asked. Example: How old are you?
- Stress questions are only used for gathering behavior about interpersonal stress tolerance and related criteria.
- Follow-up questions are asked to obtain a complete behavioral answer. Examples: How did you handle the problem? What was the result?
- Interviewers use techniques and methods that make candidates feel comfortable.
- Interviewers take detailed notes throughout the interview.
- Interviewees talk the majority of time.
- Two or more interviewers interview and evaluate each candidate.
- The same interviewers, interview all candidates for a specific opening.
- A predetermined candidate rating procedure is used.
- Enough time is scheduled for each interview and its evaluation; consequently, the interviews are not rushed.
- Interviewers do not make quick judgments about candidate suitability. Judgments are made only after a thorough post-interview evaluation is completed.
- Interviewers do not let biases and stereotypes distort their candidate evaluations.
- Candidates are rated against the selection criteria and not against each other.
- Interviewers reach a consensus evaluation on each candidate, after first making independent evaluations.

- Pressure to fill the position leading to selecting unsuitable candidates, is resisted.
- Behavioral background checks are completed on acceptable candidates.

Are you incorporating the above practices in your interviewing? If so, great, keep it up. If not, the information presented in this guide will help you improve your interviewing practices. As a result, you and your organization will benefit by hiring good performers more often. In addition, you will incur, less often, the very significant monetary and emotional costs associated with hiring or promoting marginal and poor performers.

QUIZ: TEST YOUR KNOWLEDGE ABOUT BEHAVIORAL INTERVIEWING.

Are the following questions behavioral questions? Yes or No? Place a mark in the appropriate column.

	Yes	No
1. Describe your strengths and weaknesses.	___	___
2. Why should we hire you?	___	___
3. How many days were you absent last year?	___	___
4. How resourceful are you?	___	___
5. What is your dream job?	___	___
6. Tell us about your future career objectives.	___	___
7. Describe a time when you received recognition for a work improvement idea you suggested.	___	___
8. Do you show co-operation on the job?	___	___
9. What would you do if you saw a fellow employee steal?	___	___
10. What do you think of the phrase "no risk, no reward?"	___	___
11. Tell us about a time when you had a conflict with a co-worker.	___	___

12. Describe a situation where delegation is not an option. ___ ___

Are the following statements True or False?   True False
13. On average, a good worker does twice as much work as a poor worker. ___ ___
14. A structured interview means asking the questions in exactly the same way for all interviewees. ___ ___
15. It is necessary to take verbatim notes in an interview? ___ ___
16. The monetary value added of a high performer is equivalent to half of their yearly salary. ___ ___
17. Untrained managers, with good people skills, interview as effectively as trained interviewers. ___ ___
18. A company can be sued for not checking a candidate's employment related background. ___ ___
19. Behavioral interviewing concentrates on observing the interviewee's behavior during the interview. ___ ___
20. A good interviewer should ignore his/her "gut" feelings about an interviewee. ___ ___

Correct answers: (1) N (2) N (3) Y (4) N (5) N (6) N (7) Y (8) N (9) N (10) N (11) Y (12) N (13) T (14) F (15) F (16) F (17) F (18) T (19) F (20) F

PLEASE NOTE: DON'T WASTE YOUR TIME READING THIS GUIDE IF YOU ARE NOT REALLY TRYING TO HIRE OR PROMOTE THE MOST QUALIFIED PERSON FOR THE JOB.

Who wouldn't be interested in hiring or promoting the most qualified? Unfortunately, there are numerous situations where hiring or promoting the most qualified candidate is not the objective. Some of these situations are:

- A friend or relative will be given the job.

- A person will be given the job to secure a benefit.
- One candidate will be given the job as a reward for dedicated service.
- The candidate with the most seniority will be given the job.
- The minority candidate will be given the job to meet a mandatory or voluntary affirmative action program requirement.
- A poorly qualified candidate will be hired by an incompetent Manager to avoid being "shown-up."
- The most attractive candidate will be given the job.
- A candidate will be hired based on a strongly held, yet unproven, bias or stereotype.

BEHAVIORAL INTERVIEWING GUIDE

A Practical, Structured Approach
For Conducting Effective
Selection Interviews

PAST BEHAVIOR IS THE BEST PREDICTOR OF
FUTURE BEHAVIOR

TOM S. TURNER

CANADA　　　UK　　　IRELAND　　　USA　　　SPAIN

© Copyright 2004 Tom S. Turner
All rights reserved. No part of this publication may be reproduced, stored in a retrieval system, or transmitted, in any form or by any means, electronic, mechanical, photocopying, recording, or otherwise, without the written prior permission of the author.

Note for Librarians: a cataloguing record for this book that includes Dewey Decimal Classification and US Library of Congress numbers is available from the Library and Archives of Canada. The complete cataloguing record can be obtained from their online database at:
www.collectionscanada.ca/amicus/index-e.html
ISBN 1-4120-4285-2
Printed in Victoria, BC, Canada

TRAFFORD

Offices in Canada, USA, Ireland, UK and Spain
This book was published on-demand in cooperation with Trafford Publishing. On-demand publishing is a unique process and service of making a book available for retail sale to the public taking advantage of on-demand manufacturing and Internet marketing. On-demand publishing includes promotions, retail sales, manufacturing, order fulfilment, accounting and collecting royalties on behalf of the author.
Book sales for North America and international:
Trafford Publishing, 6E-2333 Government St.,
Victoria, BC v8t 4p4 CANADA
phone 250 383 6864 (toll-free 1 888 232 4444)
fax 250 383 6804; email to orders@trafford.com
Book sales in Europe:
Trafford Publishing (UK) Ltd., Enterprise House, Wistaston Road Business Centre,
Wistaston Road, Crewe, Cheshire cw2 7rp UNITED KINGDOM
phone 01270 251 396 (local rate 0845 230 9601)
facsimile 01270 254 983; orders.uk@trafford.com
Order online at:
www.trafford.com/robots/04-2092.html

10 9 8 7 6

ACKNOWLEDGEMENT

I would like to acknowledge and express my appreciation to William C. Byham, Ph.D. for providing me with the opportunity to acquire my initial, and very valuable, consulting experiences with the Behavioral Interview and Assessment Center selection methodologies. As an affiliate of Bill's company, Development Dimensions International, I had the opportunity to provide consulting and training services to a variety of organizations in relation to DDI's excellent Targeted Selection and Assessment Center programs. This experience provided me with a solid foundation for the application of the behavior recognition, recording, classification and rating skills that are essential to effective behavioral interviewing. Thanks Bill.

Tom Turner
August 2004

CONTENTS

1. Introduction _____ 13
2. Some Essential Selection Interviewing Information _____ 16
3. Preparing For The Interview _____ 21
4. Conducting The Interview _____ 45
5. Evaluating The Interview _____ 59
6. Background Checking _____ 66
7. Informing Candidates _____ 73

Appendices
A. Interview Guides _____ 75
B. Selection Criteria _____ 111
C. Behavioral Interview Questions _____ 114
D. Candidate Rating Sheet _____ 138
E. Background Checking Guide _____ 139

Publications and Services – Ordering Information _____ 143

CHAPTER ONE

INTRODUCTION

PURPOSE OF THIS GUIDE

The purpose of this guide is to explain and demonstrate how to effectively plan and conduct a structured, behavioral interview when hiring or promoting employees. By using the practices and techniques presented in this guide you will hire or promote good performers more often and select poor performers less often. Is it worth it? You bet! Selection research studies indicate good workers do twice as much work as poor workers. In addition, each year they are with an organization, good workers contribute a monetary value added equivalent in the range of 70% to 140% of their annual salary. (1,2,3) Better selection and interviewing practices will also significantly reduce the huge monetary and emotional costs associated with hiring and promoting poor performers. Bad decisions, equipment and material damage, accidents, customer complaints, low employee morale, legal fees, overtime wages and replacement hiring fees are just some of the substantial costs associated with hiring or promoting poor workers.

CHAPTER ONE

WHAT TYPE OF SELECTION INTERVIEW WILL BE EXPLAINED IN THIS GUIDE?

This guide explains how to prepare, conduct and evaluate a **structured, behavioral interview**. As explained in the next chapter, this is the best type of selection interview to use. Also incorporated into this guide are the interviewing elements of:
- predetermining selection criteria.
- using a team or panel of interviewers.
- using an interview guide.
- using a quantitative rating scale to evaluate candidates.
- completing behavioral background checks before making a final decision.

All of the above noted elements increase the effectiveness and validity of the selection interview. You can be very confident that the interviewing approach presented in this guide is valid and practical. Please note that a structured, behavioral interview **is not** a situational interview, nor is it a stress interview or an unstructured interview. These types of selection interviews are very different and significantly less valid.

HOW THIS GUIDE IS ORGANIZED?

Chapter two contains some essential information that good selection interviewers need to know. The subsequent chapters are presented in the same chronological order as an interview is normally completed. Chapter three concentrates on preparing for the interview, including selection criteria identification and behavioral question formulation. The fourth chapter focuses on conducting the interview, using a structured guide and other effective interview techniques. Chapter five explains how to evaluate the interview and chapter six focuses on conducting behavioral background checks. Chapter seven contains some suggestions and considerations for informing candidates of their interview results.

The four appendices contain listings of common selection criteria, possible behavioral interview questions, an example candidate rating sheet and an example of a background checking guide.

REFERENCES:

1. Schmidt, F L & Hunter, J E (1983) Individual differences in productivity: an empirical test of estimates derived from studies of selection procedure utility. *Journal Of Applied Psychology*, 68, 407-414.
2. Schmidt, F L, Gast-Rosenberg, I & Hunter, J E (1980) Validity generalisation results for computer programmers. *Journal Of Applied Psychology*, 65, 643-661.
3. Schmidt, F L & Hunter, J E, McKenzie, R C, & Muldrow, T W, (1979) Impact of valid selection procedures on work-force productivity. *Journal Of Applied Psychology*, 64, 609-626.

CHAPTER TWO

ESSENTIAL SELECTION INTERVIEWING INFORMATION

THE SELECTION INTERVIEW AS AN ASSESSMENT METHOD

The selection interview is one of many assessment methods being used to determine a person's suitability for hiring or promotion. Other commonly used methods are:

- Tests – intelligence, aptitude, integrity, knowledge.
- Inventories – personality, interest, values, attitudes, opinions.
- Simulations – used individually or in the context of an assessment center.
- Physical fitness assessments.
- Peer appraisals.
- Subordinate appraisals.
- Background checks.

What concerns the potential user of these various assessment methods is how good are they at picking the most qualified candidate. Predictive validity is the measure used to evaluate how good an assessment method is at picking good performers. Research indicates that a ***structured, behavioral interview***, if it is done correctly, can achieve a superior level of predictive validity when compared with other types of interviews and other assessment methods. (1,2,3,4,5) This guide explains how to prepare and conduct a structured behavioral interview. Use the best, to select the best.

Selection research results indicate that using two or more assessment methods can produce better predictive validity than one assessment method alone. Therefore, you may want to **consider supplementing the structured behavioral interview with one or two other assessment methods** to achieve even better selection results. Two good combinations to consider are: a) the interview and mental ability testing, and; b) the interview and integrity testing. Combining all three methods would be another good option.

TYPES OF INTERVIEWS

There are a variety of interview formats being used for hiring and promotional purposes. Some of the more commonly used formats are:

- Structured or patterned – a step-by-step approach, with the majority of questions predetermined.
- Behavioral – questions are asked that provide information about the candidate's past or current behavior.
- Stress – questions are asked, or statements made, to put the candidate under stress and observe how they respond.
- Unstructured – a free-flowing approach with no predetermined steps or questions.
- Screening – usually a relatively short (10-15 minutes) phone or face-to-face interview used to ensure candidates meet the "must have" criteria and to eliminate obviously unsuitable applicants.
- Situational – asking predetermined situational questions. (Example: What would you do if you had a serious conflict with your Supervisor?)

The first two formats, structured and behavioral, are the best ones to use.

Chapter Two

WHAT MAKES AN INTERVIEW VALID?

In addition to *using a structured, behavioral format*, what other elements should be included in the interview to increase its validity and effectiveness?

Research results and extensive experience leads us to suggest you include the following practices in your selection interviewing:

- Focus the interview on job related success criteria.
- Use a job-related interview guide document.
- Prepare and ask job related behavioral questions.
- Use two or more interviewers to interview each candidate. (6)
- Use a predetermined evaluation and decision making process.
- Take thorough notes and use them extensively when evaluating the candidate. (7)
- Use the same interviewers for all candidates. (8)
- Use trained interviewers. (9)
- Complete behavioral background checks to corroborate, discount or supplement the information gathered in the interview.

Each additional "best" practice introduced will increase the interview validity and effectiveness. The content of this guide incorporates all of the above bulleted practices.

THE BEHAVIORAL INTERVIEW PARADIGM

Thucydides, a famous historian said, " that it is in very nature of humans to act in the future as they did in the past."(10)

The paradigm or foundation upon which the behavioral interview rests is that *past behavior is the best predictor of future behavior.* In other words, how a person has behaved in the past will, most likely, be the way they will behave in similar situations in the future. If a person has shown honesty in the past, he or she will most likely show honesty in the future. If they have shown good teamwork, initiative and innovation in past jobs, they will most likely show the same behaviors in future jobs. If they have shown poor work standards in past jobs, then they most likely will show them in future jobs. For the vast majority of the population, the behavioral interview paradigm is accurate. Consequently, *it is the only assessment and interviewing paradigm that makes practical sense.*

UNIONIZED WORK ENVIRONMENTS

In union certified work places, the collective agreement and letters of understanding may contain clauses that impact hiring and promotional decisions. If the clauses are compatible with the information presented in this guide, there will be little or no negative impact on selection accuracy. If however, the collective agreement contains clauses that conflict with or limits the organization's ability to use good selection interviewing practices, then the negative impact will be significant and, most likely, a lot of selection mistakes will result. Unfortunately, in our experience, this is an all to common occurrence. The individuals who write selection related clauses for collective agreements, however well intentioned, are not normally knowledgeable about selection methods and their validity. The only remedy is to try and change the negative collective agreement clauses to make them compatible with good selection practices.

Now that we have presented some essential interview information we are ready to concentrate on how to effectively prepare for the structured, behavioral interview. The next chapter explains the important preparation tasks.

REFERENCES:

1. Wiesner, W H, & Cronshaw, S F, (1988) A meta-analytic investigation of the impact of the interview format and degree of structure on the validity of the employment interview. *Journal Of Occupational Psychology*, 61, 275-290.

CHAPTER TWO

2. Huffcutt A I & Arthur W (1994) Hunter & Hunter (1994) revisted: interview validity for entry-level jobs. *Journal Of Applied Psychology*, 79, 184-190.
3. McDaniel, M A, Whetzel, D L, Schmidt, F L & Maurer, S D (1994) The validity of employment interviews: a comprehensive review and meta-analysis. *Journal Of Applied Psychology*, 79, 599-616.
4. Pulakos, E D & Schmitt, N (1995) Experienced-based and situational interview questions: studies of validity. *Personnel Psychology*, 48, 289-308.
5. Campion, M A, Campion, J E & Hudson, J P (1994) Structured interviewing: a note on incremental validity and alternative question types. *Journal Of Applied Psychology*, 79, 998-1002.
6. Huffcutt, A I & Woehr, D J (1995) Further analyses of employment interview validity: a quantitative evaluation of interview related structuring methods. *Journal of Organizational Behaviour.*
7. Ibid
8. Ibid
9. Conway, J M, Jako, R A & Goodman, D F (1995) A meta-analysis of interrater and internal consistency reliability of selection interviews. *Journal Of Applied Psychology*, 80, 565-579.
10. The Peloponnesian War. Oxford, Clarendon Press, 1966, I-XXII, 4.

CHAPTER THREE

PREPARING FOR THE INTERVIEW

IMPORTANT EXPLANATORY NOTE

Structured interviews produce better results than unstructured interviews. One way to provide interview structure is to prepare and *use an Interview Guide.* In Appendix A, we have provided two generic Interview Guides. The *first guide can be used for non-management positions* and the *second one can be used for management or supervisory positions.* Please review the contents of these two generic guides before reading further. Doing so, will help to facilitate your understanding of the ideas and suggestions presented in the chapter.

While reviewing the generic Interview Guides, you will have noticed they contained the following major sections or parts:
- A preparation checklist.
- Suggested interview steps and timing.
- Suggested content for opening the interview.
- A page to note the questions to ask the candidate about their application materials and a place to record the answers.
- A section used to verify the attainment of any prerequisite educational, training and experience criteria.

Chapter Three

- An area to note contact information about previous employment supervisors.
- A number of selection criteria pages, each one containing:
  - The selection criterion name and its definition.
  - Four behavioral questions, with space between each one for recording the candidate's answers.
  - An area to note observed oral communication behaviors.
- Suggested content for closing the interview.
- A candidate evaluation page for recording interview ratings and making final evaluations.

A number of the interview preparation steps we will suggest refer to the various sections of the two generic Interview Guides.

THE INTERVIEW PREPARATION TASKS

The preparation tasks explained below are based on the assumption that a review of the application materials has been completed and that a brief screening interview has been conducted with each candidate. Such an initial phone or in-person screening interview is done to ensure candidates have met the "must have" educational, certification, experiential and training requirements as well as to confirm whether or not they would be willing to accept the established compensation range and the normal working conditions, such as shift work, weekend work, travel etc. The result of such an initial screen will be a short list of candidates that are scheduled for an in-depth interview of the type explained in this guide.

To ensure a thorough job of preparing for the in-depth, structured, behavioral interview, the following tasks need to be completed:

1. Determine the interview format and select the interviewer(s).
2. Establish the interview focus by identifying and defining the required selection criteria.
3. Prepare the interview questions and Interview Guide.

4. Determine how the rating scale will be used and how the calculations will be done.
5. Determine the interviewer roles and question sequencing (for team or panel format only).
6. Schedule the interviews and book an interview room.
7. Read the candidates application materials.

FIRST PREPARATION TASK: DETERMINE INTERVIEW FORMAT AND SELECT THE INTERVIEWER(S)

There are a multitude of interview formats you can use. Possible formats include a single interviewer, a series of single interviewer interviews, a multi-person panel or team interview and various other formats. In deciding which format you will use, keep in mind that research results indicate a panel or team interview format is a better choice than the single interviewer format. In selection interviewing, two heads are definitely better than one.

If you decide to go with a panel or team interview format the optimum size is difficult to pin down. Unfortunately, the research is inconclusive on the best panel size. Our experience tells us that a panel or group interview should not involve more than six interviewers. This number is assuming all panel members will be asking questions. If some interviewers will only be auditing the process and not asking questions, then the number of interviewers present is limited only by space and the potential negative impact on the interview atmosphere.

Recommendation

Use a team or panel of at least two and preferably three interviewers. If feasible, have the team interview all the candidates being considered. We also recommend that all interviewers participate in the planning, conducting and evaluating stages of the interview and, if you have a choice, to avoid non-participating auditors/observers.

Chapter Three

In determining the interviewers, keep in mind that research studies indicate that trained and experienced interviewers do a better job than untrained, inexperienced interviewers. (1) Some interviewer possibilities are:
- The direct Supervisor of the vacant position.
- Other organizational Supervisors and Managers .
- Human Resources Department personnel.
- Future peers or co-workers of the successful candidate.
- A future customer or client of the successful candidate.
- A Union Representative.
- An external Management Consultant or Psychologist.

If you are assessing a candidate's job specific technical knowledge in the interview, then the interviewer, or in the case of a panel, at least one of the interviewers, must be able to assess the accuracy of the technical question responses.

Some additional factors to consider when selecting interviewers are:
- Degree of objectivity desired. The more objectivity you want, the more you will use uninvolved Managers, Management Consultants and Psychologists.
- Labour contract provisions or organizational policies may state which parties are to participate as interviewers.
- "Political" considerations may play a role. For example, you may want at least one of the interviewers to be a minority group member if there are minority group candidates.
- The type of management culture you are trying to implement. For example, a self-directed team strategy normally suggests the use of incumbent team members as interviewers.
- The amount of interview training and experience required.
- The organizational level of the vacant position. Normally the interviewers are on a higher or at least equal organizational level than the vacant position.

Recommendation

Ensure that all interviewers have been well trained, particularly in behavioral interviewing techniques.

Regardless of whether you decide to go with a single interviewer or a team of interviewers, the following additional preparation tasks need to be completed.

SECOND PREPARATION TASK: DETERMINE THE INTERVIEW FOCUS BY IDENTIFYING AND DEFINING THE REQUIRED SELECTION CRITERIA

This task is absolutely essential and should not be skipped. It provides the required focus for the interview, avoids a lot of common problems and adds a great deal of validity to the interview.

By **selection criteria** we mean **those abilities, skills, personal attributes, knowledge areas, experience, education and/or training that are essential for success in the target position.** Success criteria make the difference between a very good performer and an average performer.

Other commonly used terms for selection criteria are competencies, qualifications, dimensions and job requirements. The term competency needs some comment. In our experience, most defined competencies include a broad spectrum of knowledge, skills and personal attributes. Consequently, if your interview is focused on a number of competencies you may be indirectly trying to assess twenty or more skills and attributes, which we feel, is asking too much of the interview. We feel it is better to focus on eight to twelve specific criteria (knowledge, skills, abilities and personal attributes) that are critical for success. Such a focus makes the interview more manageable, as well as more valid. More than likely, these success criteria will be required in most of the position's competency clusters. In our judgment, competencies are best suited for training and development applications and less suited for selection purposes.

Chapter Three

By focusing the interview on the success criteria that are correlated with good job performance you will always be focused on what is important and, consequently, you will make better decisions. Focusing on selection criteria will also prevent one of the most common interviewing errors, that is, collecting and considering information that is not related to good job performance. Another important advantage of focusing on success criteria is that the process will be job related and, therefore, non-discriminatory.

Types Of Selection Criteria

To help interviewers identify and define selection criteria, it is sometimes helpful to have a categorization system to use. There are many categorization systems in use. We suggest you consider the following categories:

- **Knowledge areas** – the specific knowledge that a candidate needs to bring to the job to be successful.
  Examples: financial ratios, spread sheet software, design principles, equipment operation procedures, laws/regulations etc.
- **Abilities and skills** needed for success.
  Examples: report writing, presentation skills, listening, planning, delegation, mechanical ability, etc.
- **Personality attributes** that correlate with success.
  Examples: honesty, integrity, flexibility, work standards, stress tolerance, initiative, etc.
- **Experience** – the type and amount of experience required for success
  Examples: 3 years experience as a Supervisor, 5 years contract negotiation experience, 3 years desktop publishing experience, etc.
- **Education and/or certifications** – the type and amount of formal education required or what specific certification, registration or professional designation is required to be successful.

Examples: Bachelor of Science in Computer Systems Design, trades certification as an Electrician, certification as a Professional Management Consultant, vocational school graduation in fabric design, etc.
- **Training** – what type and amount of training (shorter duration educational experiences) is required for success.
Examples: first aid, selection interviewing, internet research, time management, strategic planning, etc.

For interviewing purposes, the normal number of selection criteria would be in the range of eight to twelve. Too many and the interview process will be onerous and too few criteria will mean important information will be missed.

For your reference and possible use, **Appendix B** *lists some commonly used selection criteria.*

Legal Considerations Concerning Selection Criteria

Interviewers need to be knowledgeable about the federal, state/provincial laws and regulations that impact on selection interviewing and other aspects of the selection processes. Such legislation can potentially impact the:
- Content of the job postings and advertisements.
- Selection criteria identified for the position.
- Questions asked in the interview.
- Information used to assess candidates.
- Information gathered in a background check.

In general, selection related laws state that the selection criteria, interview questions and information gathered in background checks has to be **job related**. Job related means, that any selection criteria, interview question and elicited background information **should be related to successful job performance**. If you can demonstrate the job relatedness of a selection criterion then you have what is referred to as a **bona fide occupational qualification/requirement (B.F.O.Q/R.)**. If your entire selection process, and

Chapter Three

specifically the interview, is focused on BFOQ/R's then you can use them as selection criteria, ask questions about them, assess them and collect background information about them and not have to worry about being discriminatory. In addition, you have the peace of mind of knowing you are focused on the most important knowledge, skills, abilities and personal attributes.

Although there are some inclusion differences between federal, state and provincial laws, they all list "protected classes" or "prohibited areas". The classes or areas most often listed are: age, gender, religion, physical or mental handicap, marital status, place of origin, ancestry, race, color, criminal record, family status, sexual orientation and military service. When determining selection criteria, asking interview questions and gathering background information, avoid these areas or you could be accused of discrimination and subject to possible complaints or lawsuits. Although you should be aware of the legal requirements, if you have developed a good selection process and identified job related selection criteria you should have no problem with the legalities. In fact, you want, and need to be focused on, the job related success criteria in order to select the most qualified candidate.

Methods Of Identifying And Defining Selection Criteria

How do you go about determining the success selection criteria? There are a number of methods in common use:

- Read the position description and pick out the criteria needed to successfully complete the job tasks. For example, if the position description includes "plan and complete projects assigned" then possible success criteria are planning and organizing skill, interpersonal skills, project management knowledge, leadership ability and report writing.
- Ask the direct Supervisor of the target position what criteria their experience tells them are required for success.
- Ask incumbents of the position what success criteria are needed.

- Ask peers and workmates what success criteria are essential.
- Plan and conduct a "critical incident" meeting with individuals familiar with the position. Present and discuss both good and bad, past critical incidents. Analyze the incidents for possible success criteria.
- Select from a list of commonly used success criteria. (Appendix B)
- Select an initial list of criteria, put them in a questionnaire format, distribute it to people familiar with the target position and ask them to evaluate the importance of the list and make whatever modifications they feel are appropriate.

Recommendation

If the interview you will be conducting is a "one-shot deal" or you do not anticipate repeating the same interview process for some time, then use the methods of; 1) review of job description and/or; 2) select from a list. Remember, two heads are better than one, so elicit input from all the interviewers and other people who are familiar with the vacant position.

If you will be frequently interviewing and selecting people for the position under consideration, use as many methods as you can to identify your selection criteria. The more methods you use and the more people you involve, the greater will be your confidence that you have identified and defined the critical success criteria. In other words, take a lot of time initially to make sure you have a solid list of selection criteria upon which to focus your interviews and other parts of the selection process.

CHAPTER THREE

Core Selection Criteria

Selection research studies and our experience indicate that **for many positions, certain criteria are almost always related to success. We call these criteria "core selection criteria."** These are the "must have" knowledge areas, skills, abilities and personal qualities. The names of these core success criteria are listed below for easy reference. Their complete definitions are contained in Appendix B, as well as in the two generic Interview Guides presented in Appendix A.

For non-management positions:
- Personality Attributes – initiative, work standards, reliability, honesty, adaptability.
- Abilities And Skills – planning and organizing, interpersonal, oral communication, mental ability.
- Knowledge – job specific knowledge.

For management/supervisory positions:
- Personality Attributes – initiative, work standards, reliability, honesty, adaptability.
- Abilities And Skills – planning and organizing, interpersonal, oral communication, mental ability, delegation, control, leadership.
- Knowledge – job specific knowledge

Recommendation

When you are in the process of identifying your success criteria give careful consideration to our suggested " *core selection criteria.*" They are almost always associated with success in a position. Unless there is a very solid reason not to, include the "core selection criteria" in your list of interview criteria along with the other job specific success criteria you identify and define.

When deciding whether or not to include a specific selection criterion in your list you may want to consider the following:

- If you will be training the successful candidate in a particular selection criterion then there would be no need to include it in your list. Include only criteria that the candidate has to bring to the position. In other words, the candidate must already possess the skill, attribute or knowledge because you will not have the time and/or resources to train or coach them. Generally, it is possible to train on knowledge or skills, but is very difficult, if not impossible, to develop a missing personality attribute. In most instances, the success personality attributes should be "brought to the game."
- Is the interview the best selection method for assessing the criterion? For example, writing ability is difficult to assess in an interview. A better way to assess it would be to use a writing exercise where you ask the candidate to write a report, letter, paper, etc. The same can be said for the criterion of mechanical ability. Using commercially available mechanical ability tests is a better assessment method than the interview for this criterion.
- Do you have to ask questions about the skill or ability or can you readily observe it during the interview? For example, oral communication ability can be effectively assessed by observing the candidate's actual speaking and listening behavior during the interview.

Need Help?

Contact us if you would like us to prepare a job specific list of selection criteria along with our recommendations on which ones should be included in the interview and which ones need other assessment methods. We will require a job description and the name of a job content expert (a person very knowledgeable about the position responsibilities) we can contact.

CHAPTER THREE

THIRD PREPARATION TASK: PREPARE THE INTERVIEW QUESTIONS AND INTERVIEW GUIDE

Preparing good interview questions is a critical preparation task and one of the main factors that will determine interview validity and effectiveness. Interviewing research studies indicate that **questions designed to gather information about a candidate's past or current behavior are the best kind of interview questions to prepare and ask**. These types of questions are referred to as behavioral questions, and are prepared for each success criterion.

Using behavioral questions in an interview is based on the assumption or paradigm that a candidate's current or past behavior is the best predictor of their future behavior. For example, if a candidate showed good initiative in the past it is highly probable that they will show the same initiative in future. Some examples of behavioral questions follow:

Initiative
Tell us about a significant work improvement idea you offered your Supervisor in the last six months.

Work Standards
Describe a time when you and your Supervisor had a disagreement about your work performance.

Interpersonal Skill
Give us a specific example of how you developed an effective working relationship with a co-worker.

Leadership
Tell us about a time when your leadership made the difference between success and failure.

Behavioral questions are open-ended, requiring more than a yes or no response, and most likely, begin with words and phrases such as:

>   Tell us about...
>   Describe a time...
>   Explain to us...
>   Give us an example...
>   What were...
>   In your current job, how do you...
>   Have you...
>   Where have you...
>   How do you...
>   Why did you...
>   When did you...
>   What did you do ...

As you can determine from the above statements, often you are not really asking a question, but rather asking for specific examples of past or current behavior.

We suggest you prepare and ask behavioral questions that seek both positive and negative examples of behavior. For example, a positive question would be " Describe a time you won an award for good work performance." An example of a negatively phrased question would be "Tell us about a time when you had to disregard policy in order to get the job done." By using both negative and positive questions you get more of a balanced and accurate picture of the candidate, as well as avoiding biasing your interview toward either the positive or negative side.

Appendix C lists hundreds of **behavioral questions for the core selection criteria**, as well as for some other commonly used criteria.

CHAPTER THREE

Questions To Avoid Using

We would strongly suggest you avoid the following types of questions:

- ✗ **Leading Questions** – Leading questions essentially tell the interviewee what you want to hear. For example, "We need motivated people in our organization. Are you well motivated?" How the candidate should respond is so obvious, the question response will not add any real predictive value.

- ✗ **Theoretical Or Situational Questions** – The interviewee is presented with a situation and asked how they would respond. For example, "What would you do if you saw a co-worker steal something?" The candidate will tell you what they think they would do, but you have no way of determining if they would, in real life, actually show this behavior. Also, they may give you the theoretically correct answer, but that is no guarantee that they would actually behave that way on the job. If you assume they will do as they say, you may be making a big mistake. Hypothetical questions allow for hypothetical answers. Some people argue they also encourage the candidates to lie.

- ✗ **Illegal Questions** – Avoid questions that gather information about the prohibited/protected class areas we noted earlier in the chapter. For example, "How old are you?" or another, "Are you married?"

- ✗ **Commonly Asked Non-Behavioral Questions** – These are questions (and the answers as well) that are so frequently used they appear in almost every book, article or web site designed to help the interviewee. Since the answer will likely be "the right" or "canned" response provided by a third party, the validity of the information obtained is questionable. Some commonly asked questions are:
    - Tell us about yourself.

- What are your strengths and weaknesses?
- Where do you want to be five years from now?
- Tell us why we should hire you.
- What did you do to prepare for this interview?
- What do you know about this organization?
- Why are you applying for this job?

× **Stupid Questions** – Some interviewers have a favourite question(s) that they think provides vital information that is correlated with job success. Most likely this correlation has never been properly established and the question is simply a stupid question. Some examples we have heard are:
- Who is your favourite comedian?
- Do you salt your food before tasting it.
- Do you and your wife hold hands when you go for a walk.
- If it rained music, what would grow?
- Should Prozac be added to the water supply?
- Why are sewer covers round?

Test Your Question I.Q. – Can you readily identify a behavioral question? Take the quiz at the end of this chapter.

A Special Case: The Use Of Stress Questions

As the name suggests, stress questions put the interviewee under stress. Interviewers generally rationalize their use by saying they want to see how the candidate behaves under stress, since the job requires they have good interpersonal stress tolerance. Some examples of stress questions are:
- Why didn't you go further in school?
- All your jobs to date have been pretty menial, why is that?
- Tell us why we should hire you?
- Your application was not well done. Is this a sample of your work standards?

Chapter Three

- Persuade us that you are qualified for this position.

If interpersonal stress tolerance is a critical success criterion, and you decide to use stress questions, consider the following. First, use them toward the end of the interview. If they are used at the beginning they will have a lingering negative impact throughout the entire interview. Second, after asking the questions, explain to the candidate why you used them and apologize for putting them on the spot.

How Many Questions Per Criterion

Some selection criteria require only one question to determine if they are met. For example if the success criterion is "Must have five years experience as a Supervisor" then the question " How many years have you been a Supervisor?" will provide the information you need. Other criteria require a number of questions to provide you with enough behavioral information to make a judgment. This is particularly the case with the criteria categories of knowledge, abilities, skills and personal attributes.

Recommendation

For selection criteria requiring more than one question, prepare four questions per selection criteria, two positively phrased and two negatively phrased. Plan to ask three of the questions and keep the fourth as a back-up. Use five or six questions if the criterion is very important.

How Much Time?

On average, it takes eight to ten minutes to ask three behavioral questions and take notes of the responses. If we consider the time it takes for completing the other parts of the interview and the variation in the number of criteria, a thorough behavioral interview can take from 40 minutes to 2 hours. A realistic time for a behavioral interview with eight to ten selection criteria and three questions per criterion would be 45 minutes to 1 hour. It takes approximately 10-15 minutes to evaluate an interview.

Behavioral Interviewing Guide

Recommendation

Using the guidelines provided on page 2 of the Interview Guides(Appendix A), to estimate the amount of time needed for each interview, add 15 minutes and then use the resulting time estimate for scheduling purposes.

Need Help?

Contact us if you want a job specific list of behavioral questions prepared for your success selection criteria.

Preparing The Interview Guide

Once the selection criteria have been identified and defined and the behavioral questions developed, you can prepare your Interview Guide. Please feel free to use our generic Interview Guides as templates. Once the word processing is finished, run off as many copies as you will need (one per interviewer, per candidate) and keep a master for future use.

Need Help?

We can prepare job specific Interview Guides for your selection interview requirements. We would need a list of your selection criteria, or a job description if you wish us to develop the criteria, along with a job content expert contact that we can phone or Email.

Printed packages of the two generic Interview Guides contained in this guide can be ordered by contacting us. (see last page)

**FOURTH PREPARATION TASK:
DETERMINE HOW THE RATING SCALE WILL BE USED AND HOW THE CALCULATIONS WILL BE DONE**

In our example Interview Guides we use the 1 to 5 quantitative rating scale that is reprinted below. We have used this scale for decades and have had good success with it. If you have been using another type of quantitative scale and are comfortable with it, then

Chapter Three

by all means, continue to use it. The important requirement is to ensure all the interviewers use the same rating scale.

5 = Excellent	**A great deal** of behavior relative to the success criterion was described/noted.
4 = Good	**Quite a lot** of behavior was described/noted.
3 = Satisfactory	**An average amount** of behavior was described.
2 = Unsatisfactory	**A below average amount** of behavior was described.
1 = Poor	**Very little or no** behavior was described.

You may wish to use half ratings in the scale. Examples: 3.5; 4.5 etc.

In place of the whole number scale or .5 ratings the interviewer(s) may wish to use (+) and (-) ratings. Examples: 3+; 3-; 4- etc.

Some additional suggestions for you to consider when planning the use of the rating scale are:

- Do the evaluation immediately after the interview. The information is "fresh" at this time. Evaluation takes about 10 to 15 minutes, on average.
- Evaluate each candidate against the selection criteria and not against each other. This will ensure you get a qualified candidate and not the best of a bad lot.
- Rate each selection criterion separately and then assign an overall candidate suitability rating after the individual criterion ratings have been agreed to.
- If you are using a team or panel approach, each interviewer should do an independent rating first and then share their ratings, discuss the rationale that lead to their ratings and then, as a last step, **reach a consensus rating. Do not agree to simply average the individual interviewer ratings to achieve the final criterion rating.** Sharing individual ratings, discussing differences and achieving a consensus is definitely the best approach.

- Weight your selection criteria. In reality, selection criteria are not equal. Some criteria are more important than others and this should be reflected in the rating process. Weight the more important selection criteria by multiplying their consensus ratings by 2. Multiply very important criteria ratings by 3. All the remaining consensus ratings are multiplied by 1. For an example of how this weighting is done, refer to **Appendix D**. There are other weighting methods that can be used. If you are using one that is different from ours and are satisfied with it, then by all means continue to use it.
- Establish a minimum suitability rating the candidate has to achieve. For example, on a scale of 1 to 5, 5 being high, candidates must achieve an overall average criterion suitability rating of 3 or more to be considered for the position. Alternatively, the candidates must achieve a 3 rating or higher on each of the criterion. This guards against the error of hiring the best of a bad bunch.
- Make a decision on the candidate's overall suitability for the position before moving to the next interview. This suitability decision should be subject to a background check.
- Document your individual and consensus evaluation ratings as well as your overall suitability assessment.

FIFTH PREPARATION TASK (FOR TEAM FORMAT ONLY): DETERMINE INTERVIEWER ROLES AND QUESTION SEQUENCING

If you have decided to use a team format, the interviewers will have to decide who will open the interview, who will describe the organization and vacant position, who will close the interview and who will ask which questions. We would suggest that one team member be designated to open and close the interview and direct the questioning. This person is sometimes referred to as the Chairperson. We would suggest that the selection criteria pages and their

Chapter Three

related behavioral questions be divided equally amongst all the interviewers, including the Chairperson. Each team member would ask their three or four questions on their assigned criterion page and then direct the questioning to another interviewer and so on, alternating the questioning until all the criteria pages have been covered. To keep track of who has been assigned to ask questions on each criterion, write the team member's name on the top of the applicable Interview Guide page. In most team/panel interview formats, the candidate's questions are answered by the most qualified interviewer. For example, technical questions asked are answered by the technical expert, pay and fringe benefit questions by the Human Resource member etc.

Recommendation

Have the Team/Panel Members agree that they can ask follow-up questions on each other's questions, if they feel it is necessary in order to obtain a complete answer.

SIXTH PREPARATION TASK:
SCHEDULE INTERVIEWS, ARRANGE FOR INTERVIEW ROOM AND COPY REQUIRED DOCUMENTS

Scheduling Interviews

When scheduling the interviews, error on the side of scheduling more time rather than setting a tight schedule. As a guide, 1.5 hours is a good time for an interview with 8-10 selection criteria and three questions for each criterion. This amount of time will allow for a 10 to 15 minute evaluation and a short buffer time period.

Interview Room

Arrange for an interview room that has the following features:
- Quiet and free of interruptions and distractions.
- Comfortable seating.

- A rectangular table (not a round one). A good set up for a two or three member team/panel interview is to have the members sitting behind a four by eight table with the Chairperson in the middle. Seat the candidate directly across the table from the team, opposite the Chairperson with about six feet of distance separating them.
- Good lighting and temperature control.
- Position the furniture so that any strong outside light is coming from the side and not directly behind the interviewer(s) or candidate.
- Have pen, paper and water available for the candidates use during the interview.

Copy Required Documents

- Candidate application materials – one copy per interviewer, per candidate.
- Interview Guides – one copy per interviewer, per candidate.
- Applicant waiver forms – one copy per candidate.
  - We suggest you use a general waiver form. Such a waiver gives you the candidate's permission to check work history, education history, former Supervisors and other information provided by the candidate. The waiver can also be expanded to cover credit history, criminal record and driver record. We suggest you seek legal assistance to have a general applicant waiver form prepared to fit your organization.

SEVENTH PREPARATION TASK:
READING THE CANDIDATE'S APPLICATION DOCUMENTS.

Read over candidate's application documents and note any questions you want to ask about or additional information you will need from the candidate. There is a place on page 4 of the In-

Chapter Three

terview Guide to record these questions and to note the candidate's responses.

Review the prepared behavioral questions and modify them or prepare new questions for any that will not work with the candidate. For example, if the application documents show the person has not had any supervisory experience then any prepared questions about supervision should be substituted.

Modify the behavioral questions to better fit with the candidate's background. For example, if one of your questions began "At your last employer did you...," then substitute the actual employer's name for the phrase "your last employer."

You have done the hard work. You are now well prepared to conduct the interview. The preparation you have done will go a long way to achieving the desired end result of selecting good performers more often and avoiding hiring mistakes.

REFERENCES:

1. Conway, J M, Jako, R A & Goodman, D F (1995) A meta-analysis of interrater and internal consistency reliability of selection interviews. *Journal Of Applied Psychology,* 80, 565-579.

BEHAVIORAL INTERVIEWING GUIDE

QUESTION I.Q. QUIZ

Instructions: Read each question and determine if it is a **leading** question, a **hypothetical** question, a **behavioral** question, an **unacceptable** (illegal), or a **stress** question. Put your answer on the line opposite the question. The answers are at the end of the quiz.

1. Are you a decisive person? _____
2. How would you handle an irate client/customer? _____
3. What were your major responsibilities in your last job? _____
4. Prove to me that your interest in this job is sincere? _____
5. What are your strengths? _____
6. Tell us about a time you felt it best to bend the rules? _____
7. Describe a leader you admire. _____
8. Tell us about the most important decision you had to make last year. _____
9. How many children do you have? _____
10. Have you ever been given responsibility for planning and implementing a major project? Tell us about it. _____
11. Do you have any handicaps? _____
12. Are you steady under pressure? _____
13. With your qualifications why should we hire you? _____
14. How many overtime hours have you worked this month? _____
15. Describe how you prepared for this interview. _____
16. How do you handle tension with your boss? _____

Chapter Three

17. Will your family obligations prevent you from doing overnight travel?   _____
18. Where would you like to be five years from now?   _____
19. Do you like to supervise others?   _____
20. Why have you held so many low status jobs?   _____

Answers: (1) leading (2) hypothetical (3) behavioral (4) stress (5) hypothetical (6) behavioral (7) hypothetical (8) behavioral (9) unacceptable (10) behavioral (11) unacceptable (12) leading (13) stress (14) behavioral (15) behavioral (16) hypothetical (17) unacceptable (18) hypothetical (19) leading (20) stress.

CHAPTER FOUR

CONDUCTING THE INTERVIEW

INTRODUCTION

Now that you have completed your preparation for the interview you are ready to conduct the interview. We suggest you use the following steps to guide you through the interview. (These steps are also included in the content of the two Interview Guides presented in Appendix A)
- Open the interview.
- Ask the questions you have from the reading of the candidate's application documents and note the candidate's responses.
- Ask your prepared behavioral questions for each selection criterion.
- If appropriate, provide information about the vacant position and your organization.
- Ask the candidate if they have any questions and provide the answers.
- Close the interview.

Research studies indicate that structured interviews are more valid. Following the above steps in each interview is one way of providing structure to the interview. Other ways of providing structure

Chapter Four

are to use predetermined criteria, prepared questions and an agreed upon rating scale. As noted in the last chapter, using an Interview Guide will also provide structure to the interview. If you have completed the preparation tasks explained in the last chapter, you have already incorporated all of the above structure elements into your interviewing.

The rationale for each of the suggested conducting steps follow. Later on in the chapter, we also address some common situations encountered in the interview and provide suggestions for handling them.

**FIRST STEP:
OPEN THE INTERVIEW**

We suggest you cover the following points in your opening. (These points are incorporated in the generic Interview Guides – Appendix A.)

- Introduce yourself and the other interviewers present. Include your position titles and how you prefer to be addressed.
- Explain the purpose of the interview. Example: "This interview will give us an opportunity to ask questions about your background and qualifications in order to make a fair evaluation of your suitability for the position of _____. It will also give you an opportunity to ask us questions about the position and organization so you can determine if your needs and expectations would be met."
- Explain the steps you will follow and how long it will take. Example: "Initially we will ask you questions about your application documents. We will then continue with questions we have prepared in relation to our selection criteria for the position. After we finish our questions we will briefly describe the position for you and answer any questions you have. We will then close the interview by explaining when

we will get back to you with our decision. This interview should take approximately one hour."
- Tell the candidate you will be taking notes throughout the interview to ensure a thorough and fair evaluation.
- Explain that all the interviewers will share in the asking of questions and they will all take notes. Explain to the candidate that they can take notes using the paper and pen provided. Invite them to help themselves to water at any time throughout the interview.
- Ask the interviewee if everything is clear, if they are comfortable and if they are ready to proceed.
- Make a transition comment to the next step. Example: "Lets start by covering the questions we have about your application documents."

SECOND STEP:
ASK THE QUESTIONS YOU HAVE FROM THE READING OF THE CANDIDATE'S APPLICATION DOCUMENTS AND NOTE THEIR RESPONSES AND COMMENTS.

First, ask the questions you have about the candidate's application documents. The answers they provide can sometimes influence whether or not you will ask a prepared question or can often influence how you phrase your questions. The candidate's responses can also raise unanticipated questions that need answering before you continue.

If the candidate has provided reference names, be sure to ask who they are and why they included them. If the candidate has not provided the names of former Supervisors, ask for them at this time. There is a place on page 4 of the Interview Guides to note the former Supervisors names, positions and contact phone numbers/Email addresses. Also ask the candidate if you have their permission to contact these former Supervisors. If they ask you not to contact a certain person, be sure to ask why and note their response. If you are using a general waiver form, have the candidate read and sign it.

THIRD STEP:
ASK YOUR PREPARED BEHAVIORAL QUESTIONS IN THE PLANNED ORDER.

This step provides a lot of the structure to the interview and keeps it focused on the success criteria. At times, the question order will need to change because of information gathered earlier in the interview. In addition, some questions will need to be omitted because they have already been answered or are no longer relevant.

An important consideration in this step is to ensure you obtain complete behavioral responses to your questions. Techniques for doing so are explained later in this chapter. If the candidate cannot think of a response to your question, give them a few minutes to think of one. If they are still unable to provide a response after a suitable period of time, move on to the next question.

FOURTH STEP:
PROVIDE INFORMATION ABOUT THE VACANT POSITION.

If appropriate, describe the vacant position responsibilities and other important features such as working conditions, team members, compensation, benefits etc. An explanation of the organizational purpose, products/services and structure is often included. It may not be necessary to complete this step if you have provided this information or will be providing it, in some other manner or if the candidate is already familiar with the position, as is often the case in a promotional competition.

FIFTH STEP:
ASK THE CANDIDATE IF THEY HAVE ANY QUESTIONS AND PROVIDE THE ANSWERS.

Interviewing is a two way street. The candidate may need information about the position and organization in order to determine their suitability and assess whether or not the position would meet their needs and expectations.

If you are using a panel format, have the most qualified interviewer answer the candidates questions. If you do not have the answer or information requested, commit to providing it later. It is a good practice to record any questions asked by the candidate on the "Interview Close" page of the Interview Guide. This will help you be more prepared for future interviews and it may provide additional behavioral information that you can use when evaluating the candidate.

Some interviewers describe the position and take candidate questions before they ask their prepared questions. We do not recommend this approach. We feel it is more important to obtain your information first. If you have scheduled back-to-back interviews, encounter other time constraints or if the candidate is inquisitive and loquacious you could find yourself running out of time with very little information gathered, if you allow the candidate to ask questions first. Consequently, your candidate evaluation accuracy will be negatively impacted.

SIXTH STEP:
CLOSE THE INTERVIEW

We suggest covering the following points in your close:
- Explain how the interview information will be processed and evaluated.
- If applicable, explain the next step in the selection process.
- Tell the candidate when they can expect the results of their interview.

Chapter Four

- Thank the candidate for the taking the interview and showing interest in the vacant position and your organization.

The previously described six steps provide the "how to" or road map for conducting the interview. In addition to the road map, there are some necessary techniques you will need to conduct an effective interview. Some of the more important techniques follow.

**TECHNIQUE:
ASKING FOLLOW-UP QUESTIONS TO OBTAIN COMPLETE RESPONSES TO BEHAVIORAL QUESTIONS.**

Obtaining complete behavioral question responses is one of the more important skills to incorporate into your interviewing. Often, the candidate will not give a complete behavioral answer to your question and you will have to ask follow-up questions to obtain a complete response. In our experience, we have found the **critical incident concept** to be a very helpful guideline for determining whether to ask a follow-up question or not and for deciding when you have a complete answer and therefore can proceed to your next planned behavioral question. What is a critical incident?

A critical incident has three distinct components:
- The **incident** or situation being described.
- The **actions** taken to deal with the incident or situation.
- The resulting **outcomes** of the actions.

A behavioral question asks the candidate to describe an incident from their past. Example: "Tell us about a time when you had a conflict with your Supervisor." The candidate may respond by providing the interviewer with a **description of an incident** from their past, what **actions they took** to handle the incident and **what outcomes resulted** from the actions. If the candidate does so, then they have provided a complete response because all the components of a critical incident are in the answer – incident, action and outcome. If the candidate does not include an explanation of what action they took to handle the incident and/or its resulting outcome, then the interviewer should ask follow-up questions to obtain this information to obtain a complete description of the behavioral incident.

Some common follow-up **questions for obtaining the action taken** are:
- "What action did you take?"
- "How did you handle that situation?"
- "What did you end up doing about the situation?"
- "What did you do then?"
- "What did you say?"
- "What happened next?"

Frequently used follow-up **questions for obtaining information about the resulting outcome** are:
- "How did that turn out?"
- "Were you satisfied with the results?"
- "Did it work out the way you hoped?"
- "How did it end up?"
- "What was the final outcome of the situation?"
- "How did you feel about the outcome?"

A candidate will sometimes give you the action but no result or incident. For example, they may respond with "I told my boss he made a big mistake." The interviewer should then ask follow-up questions to get details about the incident and the resulting outcome. Examples: "What was that all about?" or "Could you describe the circumstances surrounding this situation with your boss and also tell us about the final outcome?"

Sometimes you only get the outcome from the candidate's initial response and you have to ask a follow-up questions to obtain details about the incident and action components. Example: "There was a time when things turned out badly for me." The interviewer should ask follow-up questions such as "Please provide us with the details about that incident." and "What actions did you take that lead to the bad outcome?"

Chapter Four

Recommendation

Always ask follow-up questions until you to get all the components of a critical incident – incident, action and outcome. Do not leave any components out. In a panel interview format, encourage the interviewers to help one another with the follow-up questioning.

TECHNIQUE:
ASKING THE CANDIDATE FOR SPECIFIC BEHAVIORAL EXAMPLES

Often in behavioral interviewing, when you ask a question the candidate will respond with a meaningless generality. For example, say you ask the question "Tell us about a time you were recognized for a work improvement suggestion?" and the candidate responds with the generalized statement, "I have been recognized for good ideas many times." This answer is of no value, it's too general and vague. It is self-report information which cannot be evaluated because it contains no specific behavior, that is, information about what the candidate has actually said or did. In this situation, you should ask the candidate for a specific incident. Example: "Could you please give us a specific incident when you were given recognition?" When the candidate responds with a specific incident you will be able to evaluate it relative to the position under consideration. Would the behavioral incident described be exceptional for your organization or is it pretty ho hum?

Additionally, you do not have to be satisfied with only one specific incident for each question. If the selection criterion is particularly important, you may want to ask for two or three specific behavioral examples for a question. The follow-up would be "Give us another example of when you were recognized for offering an improvement suggestion."

A common occurrence in a behavioral interview is the candidate being unable to provide or recall a specific behavioral example. In such a situation, allow the candidate a few minutes to try and think of a response. If they still cannot come up with one, move on to the next question. To minimize the number of times this happens, some interviewers give the prepared behavioral questions to the candidate in advance of the interview and ask them to think of incidents in their past that would relate to the questions. Some provide the questions a few hour's in advance, others a few day's and others a few week's ahead of time. Unfortunately, the research is not conclusive on the validity impact of this practice of advance notification of questions. One thing is clear, advance notice of the question does help to eliminate or minimize the problem of the candidate not being able to think of a specific behavioral incidents.

Recommendations

Do not accept meaningless general statements for answers. Ask the candidate to give you a specific behavioral example.

Try giving out the behavioral questions in advance and evaluate the impact it has on your interviewing in general and, in particular, the candidate's ability to come up with good incident examples.

TECHNIQUE:
TAKING COMPLETE NOTES, USING KEY WORDS

As mentioned earlier in the guide, taking notes in a behavioral interview is critical. Your recorded notes provide you with the behavioral information with which to thoroughly evaluate the suitability of a candidate. The more notes the better.

Unless you are proficient at shorthand, it is virtually impossible to record everything the candidate says. One way to handle this situation is to use the shortcut technique of recording key words only and not worry about recording everything that is said. The recorded key words will be sufficient to trigger your recall of the entire incident during the evaluation stage of the interview. For example, if the candidate is describing an incident when he/she did not handle a project management situation well, your notes could be similar to the following.

Chapter Four

I – project – new database software – behind schedule

A – threatened to replace certain members

O – even less motivation – project completion overdue

You will notice that the key words in the above example are also noted opposite the letters I, A, and O, which represent the words incident, action and outcome, the components of a critical incident. A lot of behavioral interviewers find this to be an effective way to record and recall specific behavioral incidents without having to worry about getting things down verbatim. In the Interview Guides the letters I, A, O are listed under each question to facilitate note taking.

Avoid the trap of taking periodic or few notes. Record the candidate's answers continuously, from start to finish, pausing briefly to make eye contact and to show encouraging non-verbal gestures such as head nodding, smiling, leaning forward and using vocals such as "yes", "um", "okay", "ah ha". Interviewers worry needlessly about not making continuous eye contact with the candidate. They often say "I can't take notes, I have to give the interviewee my undivided attention so as not to be rude." This is a big mistake! This approach produces limited note taking, if any, and in turn leads to a very superficial, impressionistic candidate evaluation, which results in poor decision making. Interviewees expect you to take notes and you need to take notes to make a thorough evaluation.

If you use a panel format, all interviewers should take notes continuously. A lot of panel interviewers only take notes on their own questions and not on their other panel member's questions or vice-versa. This is a mistake, because it will have the effect of reducing the overall amount of behavioral information panel members will have to consider when they evaluate the candidate.

Record your notes so they are not easily read by the candidate. If the notes can be read, it often distracts the candidate. In addition, while taking notes, periodically make eye contact with the candidate so they know you are being attentive to their remarks. Interviewers should avoid the tendency to take extraneous notes about the candidate's appearance, dress and grooming, as opposed to specific question response notes. Extraneous notes can sometimes lead to uncomfortable or awkward situations if a decision is challenged and the interview notes are examined by others.

TECHNIQUE:
DEVELOPING AND MAINTAINING A POSITIVE INTERVIEW ATMOSPHERE.

By developing and maintaining a positive interview atmosphere, the candidate will feel more comfortable in the interview and consequently, will provide more information. This leads to a more thorough candidate evaluation and better decisions. What things can you do to help create a positive atmosphere?

- Set-up the interview room as suggested in Chapter 3.
- Be attentive and empathetic with your listening. When an interviewee makes a statement that expresses a feeling, either directly or indirectly, you can respond empathetically by using a word that describes the feeling. For example, if the candidate says "I did not know how to handle that situation. I had never encountered such a thing before." Underlying that message, there is a feeling of **confusion** or **uncertainty**. You can respond empathetically by saying "Those situations are **confusing** for a lot of people." Or another possible response could be "I am sure others would feel **uncertain** in that situation." Both empathetic statements would have a positive impact on the interviewee and the interview atmosphere.
- Periodically giving the candidate a sincere compliment. Some examples would be:

Chapter Four

- "That situation was very well handled."
- "I think most people would appreciate what you did."
- "That was quite an accomplishment, good for you."

- Show positive and encouraging non-verbal communication such as smiling, eye contact, leaning forward and head nods.
- Settle down a nervous candidate by being friendly, making them comfortable and starting of with easy questions.
- Periodically, use a statement that rationalizes the candidate's stated behaviour. For example, if a candidate just explained they quit their job because of the poor supervision they received, you can offer a rationalizing statement such as "Most people would probably have done the same thing." You are not really agreeing with their behavior, but relating to the rationalizing thinking process they more than likely have gone through. Some interviewers don't like to make rationalizing statements because they feel the candidate interprets it as the interviewer is agreeing with their behavior. Each interviewer has to make their own choice as to whether to use this technique or not.
- If the interview questioning produces obvious signs of stress, discomfort or embarrassment in the candidate, the interviewer can temporarily break off the questioning and move to a less sensitive questioning area. If this is done, and the information about the sensitive area is important, the interviewer should return to it before closing off the interview.

TECHNIQUE:
MANAGING THE INTERVIEW TIMING

Some candidates are very talkative and verbose. They can dominate an interview and the interviewers have a hard time getting all their questions asked. If allowed, this can produce serious time pressure and stress in the interview. It could also negatively affect the schedule and perhaps negatively impact the candidate evaluation. What can you do to handle a talkative candidate? Here are some ways:

- If the candidate is providing too much detail, interrupt them by raising your pen, excusing yourself and indicating you have enough information. Example: "Excuse me, but I think we have enough information on that incident. Lets go to another question."
- Reinforce a brief answer. This indirectly tells the candidate that a concise response is what you want. Example: "That's a good answer, you briefly described that incident, the action you took and the outcome of that action." or "That's the kind of answer we like."
- To model the type of response desired, the interviewer can concisely summarize a complete incident that the candidate has taken too long to explain. An example of this technique would be, "In short, you had a chronically absent employee (I), who did not respond to your counselling and discipline (A), so you had to fire him (O). Is this correct?"
- The interviewer can simply ask the candidate to be more concise in their responses.

For the candidate that is reluctant to provide detail and you want to keep them talking to obtain a complete answer, you may wish to use verbal probes such as "ok", "go on", "tell me more", "what happened then" and "really". You can also paraphrase what has been said. Example: "If I heard you correctly, you just said ..., did I understand the incident correctly?" All of these verbal probes can help keep a quiet candidate talking.

TECHNIQUE:
AVOIDING BAD INTERVIEWING PRACTICES

We suggest you avoid the following practices while conducting your interview:

Chapter Four

- Don't give advice to the candidate during the interview. Example: "You should not have worn that nose ring to the interview." If the candidate is rejected, guess what he/she is going to think is the reason? Keep your opinions to yourself until the evaluation stage.
- Don't tell the candidate how they are doing in the interview. You don't know how well they are doing until you have properly evaluated the candidate and checked their background. You may regret an early commitment.
- Don't talk too much. A good rule of thumb is that the interviewers talk about 25% of the time, the candidate 75%.
- Don't argue with the candidate or put them down. This type of behavior has a negative impact and most likely will lead to less information being obtained.
- Letting your initial impression of the candidate, whether positive or negative, to affect your questioning and information gathering in the rest of the interview.
- Comparing one candidate against the others instead of comparing each candidate against the success criteria.
- Ignoring negative gut feelings when a candidate's words don't fit with the behavior they are showing. Example: The candidate states that they have extensive project presentation experience but they do not speak well during the interview.

CHAPTER FIVE

EVALUATING THE INTERVIEW

INTRODUCTION

There are numerous ways to go about rating a candidate after the interview. The approaches range from very superficial to very thorough. Our experience tells us over-and-over again, that it is best to use a thorough, consistent and fair approach to candidate evaluation.

We recently had an opportunity to observe an interview evaluation meeting as part of an employee selection audit we were completing for a client. The panel had interviewed three, short-listed candidates for the position of Administrative Manager. After all interviews were complete, the interviewers met to do the evaluation. One interviewer started the meeting by saying, "Well, what do you think? I think we should go with Jean. She made a real good impression on me. Do the rest of you agree?" The three interviewers then proceeded to make some generalized statements about Jean and the other candidates and after 10 minutes decided to make the offer to Jean. This evaluation process is a good example of how not to do it. Aside from the fact that each candidate should have been evaluated immediately after their interview, it was a very superficial approach and did not include the validity factors explained in the

Chapter Five

preparation and conducting chapters of this guide. What elements should be been included in the evaluation process to ensure its effectiveness?

- Evaluate each candidate immediately after their interview.
- Rate each selection criterion independently using the agreed upon rating scale. Once all criteria are rated individually, then make an overall suitability rating.
- In a panel format, each interviewer rates the candidate independently, without discussing their ratings with the other interviewers.
- Interviewers use the classified behavior in their notes as the basis for their ratings.
- The interviewers share their independent ratings with each other, discuss the behavioral incidents they used to make the ratings and then reach a consensus rating on each selection criterion and on the candidate's overall suitability rating.
- The candidates' consensus ratings are compared against each other and a decision made as to which candidate is best suited for the position, pending a satisfactory background check.

In the next section we will explain our recommended candidate evaluation process that incorporates the above elements, as well as other factors that produce more accurate candidate evaluations. The process takes a little getting used to, but once mastered, you will be pleased with the results and you can take comfort in the fact that you are using a thorough, consistent, fair and effective approach to candidate evaluation.

In chronological order, the steps we recommend you use to evaluate a candidate are as follows.

Behavioral Interviewing Guide

First Step: Immediately after the interview, each interviewer independently reads over their recorded notes and classifies the behaviors noted as either positive or negative examples of the selection criterion under which it is listed as well as other applicable criteria.

For example, under the "Initiative" behavioral question of "Describe how you prepared for this interview.", assume the interviewer had noted the following candidate response. (Normally, the notes would be in "key word" format and not in a complete narrative format as shown below.)

(+) *"I went to the library and read all the clippings in your organization's file. I went to your web site and read about services and past year performance. I contacted Human Resources to find out who would be interviewing me and what their positions are. I also talked to two old school mates who work here about the challenges faced by the organization."*

The interviewer evaluates whether this behavior is a positive or negative example of the selection criterion "Initiative" as defined. If the interviewer considers it a positive example (as most certainly would) they would put a (+) sign beside the notes as shown in the above example. If the interviewer thought it was negative example of behavior, he/she would put a (-) sign beside the notes. The interviewer also considers whether or not the noted behavior is a positive or negative example of any of the other interview selection criteria. If the interviewer concludes that such is the case, they would write an abbreviation of the applicable criterion beside the note. For example, if the interviewer felt the above noted behavior was also a positive example of the "Work Standards" criterion, they could write "(+) W.S." beside the notes. This is the way it would look in the notes.

Chapter Five

(+)
(+) W.S.
"I went to the library and read all the clippings in your organization's file. I went to your web site and read about services and past year performances. I contacted Human Resources to find out who would be interviewing me and their positions are. I also talked to two old school mates who work here about the challenges faced by the organization."

This process of evaluating the behavior noted in an interview relative to the selection criteria is referred to as the skill of **behavior classification**.

Second Step: After all the interview notes have been classified, the interviewers, independently, read the "(+)" and "(-)" notations for the first selection criterion and make a criterion rating using the predetermined rating scale. The rating is noted in one of the "Interviewer" columns of the Candidate Evaluation page of the Interview Guide (last page). This procedure is repeated for the other selection criteria until all have been rated. The last rating made is an overall candidate suitability rating based on all of the recorded, classified and rated behavior considered in the interview. The overall rating is also noted in the Candidate Evaluation page of the Interview Guide.

For example, assume the interviewer has classified the following "Initiative" behavioral examples in the Interview Guide.
- (+) researched the organization thoroughly before interview
- (+) paid his own way through College by selling mutual funds
- (-) did not suggest any new service ideas while working at Stylex
- (+) completed cross functional team project when others bailed
- (+) confronted and dealt with poor employee problem at Excel

To rate the selection criterion of "Initiative" the interviewer considers the above noted behaviors, assesses what a typical incumbent in the vacant position under consideration would normally show on the job relative to this noted behavior and makes a rating using the agreed upon scale.

For example, using the 1 to 5 rating scale used in the Interview Guides, the interviewer would read over the above "initiative" noted behaviors, considers what a typical incumbent would show and decides that the candidate deserves a rating of (4). In other words, the interviewer is saying the candidate presented a good amount (4) of initiative behavior in the interview when compared with a typical incumbent. If the interviewer considered the noted interview behavior to be less than satisfactory when considered against a typical incumbent, then a (2) rating would be given.

Third Step: The interviewers take turns reading out their criteria ratings and their overall suitability rating. While one is reading, the other interviewers are recording the ratings in the "Interviewer" columns in the Candidate Evaluation page of the Interview Guide. Once all ratings are recorded, taking one criterion at a time, the interviewers discuss the behavioral examples they considered in making their rating and agree on a consensus rating for that criterion. Once a consensus rating is achieved on all criteria, then an overall suitability consensus rating is made. The consensus ratings are recorded on the Candidate Evaluation page of the Interview Guide.

If all the individual interviewer ratings are the same for a particular criterion, a consensus has already achieved and normally, discussion is not necessary. If the ratings are different, then a discussion is necessary to achieve consensus. This is best done by having the interviewers explain what recorded behaviors they used to make their rating. Once this information is out on the table the interviewers re-evaluate their initial ratings and go either up or down based on any new behavioral information heard. In almost all cases, this process will achieve a consensus rating. For the odd time when

Chapter Five

consensus cannot be achieved, the ratings are simply left as they are and recorded as such.

Fourth Step: *The selection criteria weights agreed upon in the preparation phase are applied to the consensus ratings, calculations made and results recorded.*

The interviewers, using the agreed upon weightings, multiply the consensus ratings by the criteria weightings to produce the final selection criteria ratings. These final product ratings are recorded in the "Final" column of the Candidate Evaluation page. Some panels or interviewers like to add up all the final criteria ratings to obtain an overall candidate score and calculate the percentage achieved.

Appendix D has an example of what the Candidate Evaluation page of the Interview Guide would look like after completing steps 2, 3 and 4.

Fifth Step: *The interviewers compare and discuss the selection criteria ratings and overall suitability ratings of all candidates and make a consensus decision as to which candidate is best suited for the vacant position.*

This step is often done with the help of a summary matrix or form where the ratings for all the candidates interviewed are on the same page, facilitating easy reference. Each interviewer is asked for their opinion and rationale as to which candidate is best suited for the position. Further discussion results in a consensus decision on which candidate is the most qualified.

The interviewers' decision is usually considered tentative, pending acceptable background checks. In most cases the candidate who is judged to be the best suited is the first to be offered the position. In a small percentage of cases, the candidate who receives the interviewers "best suited" rating is not offered the position. For example, a poor background check may be reason enough to hold back an offer to the most qualified candidate and offer it to the next best suited candidate.

Sixth Step: (Optional) The interviewers offer training and development recommendations for the candidates based on the results of the interviews.

This step is most often used in promotional interview situations and less so in initial hiring situations. Unsuccessful promotional candidates are still with the organization, so offering development recommendations, if completed, strengthens their chances for future promotions as well as strengthening the organization.

Seventh Step: The interviewers complete any applicable administrative tasks.

Some common administrative tasks are:
- Completing a master Candidate Evaluation sheet for candidate feedback and permanent filing purposes.
- Deciding who will conduct the background checks, for how many candidates and when and how they will report the results to the other interviewers. (Refer to the next chapter for our recommendations.)
- Agreeing on who will make the job offer.
- Deciding on who will contact the unsuccessful candidates.
- Assembling and filing the application documents, completed Interview Guides and master Candidate Summary sheet.

CHAPTER SIX

BACKGROUND CHECKING

INTRODUCTION

We have included this chapter on background or reference checking because of its importance. A background check is an essential supplement to the structured, behavioral interview and should not be overlooked. Completing a background check on a candidate:

- Is a good source of additional behavioral information that can corroborate or refute the behavioral information gathered in the interview.
- Enables you to verify certain information provided by the candidate, to check out gut feelings and to ask questions about incidents or situations discussed in the interview.
- Provides an opportunity to ask about job related, common failings such as drug dependency, excessive absenteeism and poor work standards.
- Provides protection against negligent or wrongful hiring law suits.

Behavioral Interviewing Guide

To help maximize the validity of the background checking process and to facilitate a smooth integration with the interview information, we recommend a behavioral format be used when checking backgrounds. Similar to the interview, the checker asks the referee to comment about the candidate's past behavior relative to the selection criteria. For example, "How many days absent did they have last year?"(reliability), "Please comment on their willingness to change."(adaptability), "Could you please comment on their integrity and honesty?" (honesty), "Were they a self-starter or did you frequently have to ask them to get on with it?"(initiative).

Generally, we suggest that you do the background check after the in-depth interview. However, as mentioned earlier, we feel it is a good practice to complete a phone, face-to-face or Email screen to verify that a candidate has the essential prerequisites and satisfies any "must have" selection criteria before an in-depth interview is scheduled. This practice can save the time and money spent on scheduling and conducting an interview only to find shortly into the interview that the candidate is missing a "must have" prerequisite and therefore unsuitable. Some people refer to this prescreening for "must have" criteria as a background check or reference check.

Recommendation

Conduct a background/reference check on the most suitable candidate first and delay doing the other candidates until you have the results of the first one. If the background on the most suitable candidate checks out and a job offer is to be made, there is no need to spend time and money doing background checks on the other candidates, assuming you are hiring or promoting only one candidate.

The following sections of the chapter we will explain more about who should do the background checking, what people to contact and what methods of communication should be used.

Chapter Six

WHO SHOULD DO THE BACKGROUND CHECK?

In general, we feel the interviewers are the best people to conduct the background check if maximum benefit is to be realized. The interviewers are in the best position to verify candidate comments, corroborate or refute interview findings and ask about common failings.

There are different ways to organize the background checking. Some interviewers split the task, each taking an equal number of employers or supervisors to contact. Another approach is for one interviewer to do all the background checks and communicate their findings to his/her fellow interviewers. In certain situations, it may be efficient to delegate the preliminary background check task of confirming the "must have" prerequisites to someone other than the interviewers.

Some organizations contract out their background checking to consultants and private security firms. Such a practice has to be evaluated carefully to ensure the service is providing the kind of behavioral information you need and that you are not inadvertently contracting out the selection of your employees to an outsider.

Recommendation

We recommend that the interviewers equally share the background checking task. Ask other support personnel to do a pre-interview, initial background screen to verify that the "must have" prerequisites and criteria are met and that application information is accurate.

WHOM TO CONTACT?

In determining which people to contact for a background check, a good guideline to use is to contact individuals who **have frequently observed the candidate's behavior relative to the selection criteria under consideration.** Normally, the more candidate behavior the referee has observed the better the background check will be. Most often this means you will be checking with past or current supervisors, colleagues and former employees. These people are sometimes listed in the application documents, but they may not be, and that is why we suggested you collect these names at the start of the interview.(Record names on page 4 of the Interview Guide) As you would expect, you generally do not receive a lot of bad reference information from referees supplied by the applicant. Consequently, you have to question the value of only checking the contacts/references supplied by the candidate. You most likely will have to contact other people in order to obtain additional behavioral information and a more balanced picture. There is no reason why you cannot check with people other than the referees supplied by the candidate without the candidate's prior approval. However, it is common courtesy and more professional to ask for the candidate's permission during the interview or if not then, before you call a referee/supervisor whose name was not provided by the candidate.

If the candidate has had very little work experience, or none at all, you could contact former teachers, professors, coaches and community association officials. Most selection criteria behavior is also shown in non-work situations and very little, if any validity is lost when non-work referees comment about the candidate's behavior.

The Human Resources Departments of the candidate's former employers, if applicable, is a source to verify positions held, dates of service and other terms of employment. Usually Human Resource Department personnel have not actually seen a lot, if any, of the candidate's actual on job behavior and therefore they are not normally a good source of success criteria behavioral information.

WHAT METHOD OF COMMUNICATION?

There are essentially four methods interviewers can use to conduct a background check. A requested **reference letter or Email message** can be asked for. Referees are often reluctant to commit themselves in writing and consequently the letters received, if they are ever provided, can be general and lack specifics about actual

Chapter Six

past behavior. Also, the letter content may not relate to the selection criteria. An interviewer can schedule a **personal visit** with the referee. This method works well if the person is relatively close. Distance usually means more time and cost. The most frequently used background check method is the **telephone.** It allows for gathering the information you need at relatively low cost and in a short period of time.

Recommendation

Use either the telephone or the face-to face interviews to complete background checks. These two methods will provide the best behavioral information.

HOW SHOULD THE TELEPHONE BACKGROUND CHECK BE DONE?

Similar to the interview, we feel the telephone background check should be completed using a structured guide that contain specifically planned questions. Having a structured guide ensures a thorough, focused and high value background check. We suggest a structured background check guide should include the following elements:

- Recording the contact's name, position, phone number and the time and date of the call.
- Introducing yourself and explaining the purpose of your call.
- Asking the referee if they have 10 to 15 minutes now or would later be better, and if so, setting a time.
- Explaining to the contact the extent to which the information they provide will remain confidential.
- Confirming factual information provided by the candidate such as positions held, tenure, responsibilities, reasons for leaving, number of employees, size of budget etc.

- Asking for behavioral information concerning each selection criterion and taking short form notes of the contact's comments. For example, if honesty, initiative and leadership were three of your selection criteria, the questions could be:
  - "Please comment on the honesty and integrity behavior you have seen."
  - "What type of initiative did they show?"
  - "Comment on their leadership skill and style."
- Asking the referee to comment on the candidate's absenteeism, punctuality and work ethic.
- Asking about drug dependencies and job related health problems
- Asking about the candidate's quality and quantity of work.
- Asking about the candidate's relations with co-workers and supervisor.
- Asking about personal hygiene.
- Asking if they would re-hire the candidate, and if they say no, ask why.
- Asking the referee for any additional information they feel is relevant.
- Asking if they know of another person you could contact to obtain additional behavioral information.
- Thanking the contact for their cooperation.
- After the telephone call, compare the contact's assessment and comments against the interview ratings for corroboration or differences. Decide if the background check is satisfactory or not.

Appendix E contains an example Background Check Guide that covers both non-management and management core selection criteria.

Chapter Six

HOW MANY BACKGROUND CHECKS?

Our suggestion is you contact as many people as necessary to establish a distinct trend that corroborates or refutes the interview ratings. This usually means two to four checks per candidate. The more people you contact, the more behavior you collect and the more confident you are in your evaluation of the candidate.

AFTER THE BACKGROUND CHECK

You have checked the background of your number one candidate. The check corroborates your interview results. After sharing your findings with the other interviewers you decide whether or not to extend an offer or make the promotion.

If the background check of the number one candidate was not good, the interviewers need to decide if they will conduct a background check on the second best candidate and not hire or promote number one. If the second ranked and all other candidates were judged to be unsuitable, then new candidates would have to be recruited and the selection process repeated.

Need Help?

We can develop a job specific Background Check Guide for you. We will need the list of selection criteria and the name of a job content expert to contact by phone or Email.

CHAPTER SEVEN

INFORMING CANDIDATES OF RESULTS

INFORMING THE SUCCESSFUL CANDIDATE

The successful candidate is contacted and a job offer is extended. Usually this is done verbally and confirmed in writing. Some common areas usually included in a verbal and written offer are the following:
- position title
- major responsibilities
- salary
- benefits
- probationary period
- location of work and/or office
- organizational structure
- direct Supervisor
- start date
- plus other important job-specific information

Since you are entering into an employment contract, we suggest you ask for legal advice as to what information should be communicated in a candidate offer.

Chapter Seven

Agree on a date for the candidate to inform you of his/her acceptance or rejection of the offer.

Recommendation

Wait until the number one candidate has accepted the job offer before informing the unsuccessful candidates. If an offer is rejected you may decide to offer another candidate the position.

INFORMING UNSUCCESSFUL CANDIDATES

The general guidelines to follow when informing unsuccessful candidates are:

- Inform them either by telephone or Email (brief) and avoid letter formats.
- Inform them that another candidate more closely matched the selection criteria set for the position and has accepted the position.
- Thank the candidate for taking the time to apply and wish them all the best in the future.
- If done by phone and the unsuccessful candidate asks why they did not get the job reply with, "another candidate more closely matched our requirements for the job." It is usually better to avoid specific details about why a candidate was rated the way they were. Communicating the specific information that lead to rejection can sometimes produce complaints and other problems.

APPENDIX A

INTERVIEW GUIDE

NON-MANAGEMENT POSITIONS

POSITION: _____

Candidate: _____ Date: _____

Past behavior predicts future behavior.

INTELLIGENT SELECTION INC
Phone: 604 . 532 . 5947;
Email: information@intelligentselection.net
Web Address: www.IntelligentSelection.net
©Copyright 2004

Appendix

ARE YOU READY TO START THE INTERVIEW???

Being well prepared significantly contributes to the effectiveness of the interview. The following tasks should be completed before starting the interview. Check to see if you have done them all.

- ❏ Completed a screening interview and/or resume review to ensure the candidate has met the vacant position's educational, certification, experiential, training and working condition requirements. Follow-up questions have been noted on page 4.
- ❏ Know the major responsibilities and duties of the position.
- ❏ Reviewed the selection criteria in this Guide for job relatedness. Added, deleted or modified the criteria as appropriate. Prepared behavioral questions for added criteria.
- ❏ Read the prepared behavioral questions in this Guide for job relatedness. Added, deleted or modified questions as appropriate.
- ❏ Prepared the required job specific knowledge questions and recorded them on page 13.
- ❏ Determined:
    - o who will open and who will close the interview?
    - o who will ask which questions and in what order?
    - o who will describe the position to the candidate?
    - o who will answer the candidate's questions?

SUGGESTED STEPS AND TIMING

The following times are an average and can vary with candidates.

Step 1 - Open the interview	2 min.
Step 2 - Ask questions about application materials	5 min.
Step 3 - Ask prepared questions and take notes	2-3 min. each
Step 4 - Describe the position	5 min.
Step 5 - Ask if candidate has questions and answer	5 min.
Step 6 - Close the interview	2 min.
Step 7 - Evaluate the candidate	10-15 min.
Average interview time with seven to ten criteria:	1 to 1.25 hours

IMPORTANT: TAKE LOTS OF NOTES – FROM START TO FINISH

OPENING THE INTERVIEW – SUGGESTED CONTENT

1. Greet the candidate, giving your name and position. If applicable, introduce the other interviewers, giving names and positions.

2. Explain the purpose of the interview.

   Suggestion: "The purpose of this interview is for both of us to get the information we need. It will give us an opportunity to ask questions about your background and experiences in order to make a fair evaluation of your application. It will also provide you with the opportunity to ask us for information that will help you decide whether or not the position meets your requirements."

3. Explain how the interview will be conducted.

   Suggestion: "Initially we will ask you questions about your application documents. We will then ask a variety of planned questions related to our predetermined selection criteria. Toward the end of the interview we will describe the position and provide the answers to any questions you may have. Closing off the interview will be the last step of the interview."

4. Explain you will be taking notes throughout the interview.

   Suggestion: "We will be taking notes throughout the interview. This will help us make a thorough and fair evaluation of your suitability for the position."

5. Explain the water and paper is for their use. Ask if there is anything more they need before starting.

Suggested transition comment: "I think we are ready to start. We will begin with some questions about your application materials."

Appendix

QUESTIONS ABOUT APPLICATION MATERIALS

Ask the questions you have noted from the review of the application materials and the initial screening interview. Remember to record the candidate's answers.

\# 1. _____

_____

Notes:

\# 2. _____

_____

Notes:

\# 3. _____

_____

Notes:

Acceptance Of Working Conditions: If not already done so in the screening interview, explain the important working conditions (shift work, weekend work, travel, overtime hours, physical requirements etc.) and ask the candidate if they can accept them. If they cannot, you may want to end the interview at this point.

Previous Supervisors: If not already provided in the application materials, ask the candidate for the names and phone numbers of their previous Supervisors and ask for permission to contact them. If they say no, be sure to ask why.

Name	Organization	Phone

Suggested Transition Comment: "Thanks for that information, now we will ask you some questions pertaining to our selection criteria."

INITIATIVE: Willingly does work without being asked or waiting for instructions; self-starting; offers suggestions for improvement; voluntarily helps others; confronts and handles problems and situations.

Using your current/past job as a reference, provide two examples of doing more than what was expected of you.

Response: I –

   A –

   O –

Tell us about a time when you made a valuable work improvement suggestion.

Response: I –

   A –

   O –

Tell us about a time when you tackled a problem or situation that others avoided or refused to handle.

Response: I –

   A –

   O –

Back-up: Tell us about a time when you felt it necessary to change the way you do your job.

Response: I –

   A –

   O –

Oral Communication (+ or -): volume ( ) grammar ( ) vocabulary ( ) rate ( ) confident ( ) eye contact ( ) concise ( ) inflection/ modulation ( ) initial impact ( ) holds attention ( )

Appendix

WORK STANDARDS: – Tasks are consistently completed in a thorough, accurate, timely and high quality manner; sets high standards for self and others; willingly spends extra time to make sure work is done well.

Tell us about a time when your work was more thorough and of better quality than your co-workers.

Response: I –

              A –

              O –

How many hours of overtime have you worked in the last three months?

Response: I –

              A –

              O –

Everyone, at one time or other has had their work criticized or rejected. Tell us about a time when this happened to you.

Response: I –

              A –

              O –

Back-up: Tell us about a time when you went beyond the norm and put in extra hours to complete a task or project.

Response: I –

              A –

              O –

Oral Communication (+ or -): volume ( ) grammar ( ) vocabulary ( ) rate ( ) confident ( ) eye contact ( ) concise ( ) inflection/ modulation ( ) initial impact ( ) holds attention ( )

RELIABILITY: Can be counted on to meet performance expectations; completes assigned tasks and projects on time; does what they say they will do; reports to work on time and has a low level of absenteeism.

How many instances of absenteeism and lateness have you had in the last year and what were the reasons?

Response: I –

A –

O –

Periodically, everyone says they will do something for a co-worker and are unable to so for some reason. Describe a time when this has happened to you.

Response: I –

A –

O –

How did your last Supervisor evaluate your performance and reliability?

Response: I –

A –

O –

Back-up: Describe a time when you were unable to complete a project or major task on time.

Response: I –

A –

O –

Oral Communication (+ or -): volume ( ) grammar ( ) vocabulary ( ) rate ( ) confident ( ) eye contact ( ) concise ( ) inflection/ modulation ( ) initial impact ( ) holds attention ( )

Appendix

HONESTY: Communicates with others in an honest and direct manner; does not distort, exaggerate or misrepresent information; does not show deceitful, manipulative, fraudulent, criminal or other unacceptable behavior; adheres to organizational policies and rules.

At times you have to bend a policy or rule to get the job done. Describe a time when you had to do this.

Response: I –

A –

O –

Tell us about a time when you were asked to compromise your principles or ethical standards.

Response: I –

A –

O –

Have you ever witnessed or been made aware of a fellow employee doing something inappropriate, unethical or illegal? Tell us about it.

Response: I –

A –

O –

Back-up: Have you every had to withhold information from your Supervisor for what you felt was a justifiable reason? If yes, tell us about the situation.

Response: I –

A –

O –

Oral Communication (+ or -): volume ( ) grammar ( ) vocabulary ( ) rate ( ) confident ( ) eye contact ( ) concise ( ) inflection/modulation ( ) initial impact ( ) holds attention ( )

ADAPTABILITY: Willingness and ability to adapt to changing conditions, processes, policies and laws; trying a different approach, option or solution when the current one is not working.

Tell us about a time when you really "dug in your heels" and refused to co-operate with a rule or policy change.

Response: I –

A –

O –

Give us an example of a time when things were not working and you seemed to have reached a dead end.

Response: I –

A –

O –

Describe some significant changes you have made in your personal life over the last two years.

Response: I –

A –

O –

Back-up: Tell us about a time when you felt it was better not to make a change when an opportunity presented itself.

Response: I –

A –

O –

Oral Communication (+ or -): volume ( ) grammar ( ) vocabulary ( ) rate ( ) confident ( ) eye contact ( ) concise ( ) inflection/ modulation ( ) initial impact ( ) holds attention ( )

Appendix

PLANNING AND ORGANIZATION – Ability to identify and structure tasks/activities for self and others to complete an assignment or project.

Explain how do you keep track of the tasks requiring your attention?

Response: I –

   A –

   O –

Have you ever been in a situation where you had too much to do and not enough time to do everything? Tell us about it.

Response: I –

   A –

   O –

Have you ever lead a project group or team? If so, tell us how you went about doing it.

Response: I –

   A –

   O –

Back-up: What types of planning and organizing do you do in your present job? What about previous jobs?

Response: I –

   A –

   O –

Oral Communication (+ or -): volume ( ) grammar ( ) vocabulary ( ) rate ( ) confident ( ) eye contact ( ) concise ( ) inflection/ modulation ( ) initial impact ( ) holds attention ( )

INTERPERSONAL SKILL: Ability to work harmoniously with others; skill at perceiving and reacting empathetically to the needs of others; treats people with consideration, sensitivity, kindness and fairness.

Tell us about a time in the last few days when you had to respond to a person empathetically.

Response: I –

               A –

               O –

Describe a time in the last year when you had a serious disagreement with a co-worker, boss or friend.

Response: I –

               A –

               O –

Have you ever had to give someone some news that impacted negatively on them? If so, please tell us about the situation.

Response: I –

               A –

               O –

Back-up: Give us a specific example of how you go about building a relationship with a co-worker based on trust and respect.

Response: I –

               A –

               O –

Oral Communication (+ or -): volume ( ) grammar ( ) vocabulary ( ) rate ( ) confident ( ) eye contact ( ) concise ( ) inflection/modulation ( ) initial impact ( ) holds attention ( )

APPENDIX

MENTAL ABILITY: Ability to identify, gather, analyze and understand information; to reach reasoned and sound conclusions, recommendations or decisions; to understand and assimilate new technology.

What was your grade point average in school and what courses were the easiest and the most difficult for you?

Response: I –

A –

O –

What has been the most difficult job related learning situation for you?

Response: I –

A –

O –

Everyone occasionally makes a bad decision, describe a time when you made such a decision.

Response: I –

A –

O –

Back-up: Describe the most difficult problem you have had to deal with in the last year.

Response: I –

A –

O –

Oral Communication (+ or -): volume ( ) grammar ( ) vocabulary ( ) rate ( ) confident ( ) eye contact ( ) concise ( ) inflection/modulation ( ) initial impact ( ) holds attention ( )

REQUIRED JOB KNOWLEDGE: The extent of the job related knowledge learned and understood.

Critical Knowledge Area: _____

    Question:

    Answer:

Critical Knowledge Area: _____

    Question:

    Answer:

Critical Knowledge Area: _____

    Question:

    Answer:

Critical Knowledge Area: _____

    Question:

    Answer:

Critical Knowledge Area: _____

    Question:

    Answer:

Oral Communication (+ or -): volume ( ) grammar ( ) vocabulary ( ) rate ( ) confident ( ) eye contact ( ) concise ( ) inflection/modulation ( ) initial impact ( ) holds attention ( )

Appendix

_____: _____
_____
_____

?_____
_____

Response: I –
            A –
            O –

?_____
_____

Response: I –
            A –
            O –

?_____
_____

Response: I –
            A –
            O –

Back-up?_____
_____

Response: I –
            A –
            O –

Oral Communication (+ or -): volume ( ) grammar ( ) vocabulary ( ) rate ( ) confident ( ) eye contact ( ) concise ( ) inflection/modulation ( ) initial impact ( ) holds attention ( )

BEHAVIORAL INTERVIEWING GUIDE

INTERVIEW CLOSE – SUGGESTED CONTENT

1. Explain to the candidate you are going to give them a question to think about and while they are doing their thinking you will look over your notes to ensure nothing has been left out.

Suggested question – "Tell us about a time when you had to make a very unpopular decision."

2. Review your notes and note any areas in need of further questioning.

3. Ask the candidate for their response to the above question and note their answer.

Response: I –

A –

O –

4. Ask any further questions you have noted and record the response(s).

5. If required, provide a description of the position.

6. Ask the candidate if they have any questions and, if so, note them below and answer them, if you can.

Candidate's questions:

7. Explain the next step in the selection process and tell them when they can expect to hear the interview results.

8. Thank the candidate for the interview.

IMPORTANT: Begin the evaluation process immediately after the close. Do not start a second interview before completing this candidate's evaluation.

APPENDIX

CANDIDATE EVALUATION

Rate the candidate on each selection criterion. If a team format has been used it is very important that each interviewer independently rate the candidate first, then, afterwards, share those individual ratings with other team members and reach a consensus rating. Suggested rating scale:

5. A great deal of the criterion behavior was noted. **Excellent**
4. Quite a lot was described. **Good**
3. A satisfactory or average amount was described. **Satisfactory**
2. Only a small amount was noted. **Less than satisfactory**
1. Little or no behavior was described in the interview. **Poor**

CRITERIA	INTERVIEWER RATINGS			CON-SENSUS	WEIGHT-ING	FINAL
	1	2	3			
Initiative						
Work Standards						
Reliability						
Honesty						
Adaptability						
Planning & Organization						
Interpersonal Skill						
Oral Communication						
Mental Ability						
Job Knowledge						
				Overall Rating:		

INTERVIEWERS:

_____, _____, _____

Areas To Follow-up On During The Background Check:

_____
_____
_____

INTERVIEW GUIDE

MANAGEMENT/SUPERVISORY POSITIONS

POSITION: _____

Candidate: _____ Date: _____

Past behavior predicts future behavior.

INTELLIGENT SELECTION INC
Phone: 604 . 532 . 5947;
Email: information@intelligentselection.net
Web Address: www.IntelligentSelection.net
©Copyright 2004

APPENDIX

ARE YOU READY TO START THE INTERVIEW???

Being well prepared significantly contributes to the effectiveness of the interview. The following tasks should be completed before starting the interview. Check to see if you have done them all.

- ❑ Completed a screening interview and/or resume review to ensure the candidate has met the vacant position's educational, certification, experiential, training and working condition requirements. Follow-up questions have been noted on page 4.
- ❑ Know the major responsibilities and duties of the position.
- ❑ Reviewed the selection criteria in this Guide for job relatedness. Added, deleted or modified the criteria as appropriate. Prepared behavioral questions for added criteria.
- ❑ Read the prepared behavioral questions in this Guide for job relatedness. Added, deleted or modified questions as appropriate.
- ❑ Prepared the required job specific knowledge questions and recorded them on page 16.
- ❑ Determined:
    - o who will open and who will close the interview?
    - o who will ask which questions and in what order?
    - o who will describe the position to the candidate?
    - o who will answer the candidate's questions?

SUGGESTED STEPS AND TIMING

The following times are an average and can vary with candidates.

Step 1 - Open the interview	2 min.
Step 2 - Ask questions about application materials	5 min.
Step 3 - Ask prepared questions and take notes	2-3 min. each
Step 4 - Describe the position	5 min.
Step 5 - Ask if candidate has questions and answer	5 min.
Step 6 - Close the interview	2 min.
Step 7 - Evaluate the candidate	10-15 min.
Average interview time with seven to ten criteria:	1 to 1.25 hours

IMPORTANT: TAKE LOTS OF NOTES – FROM START TO FINISH

BEHAVIORAL INTERVIEWING GUIDE

OPENING THE INTERVIEW – SUGGESTED CONTENT

1. Greet the candidate, giving your name and position. If applicable, introduce the other interviewers, giving names and positions.

2. Explain the purpose of the interview.

Suggestion: "The purpose of this interview is for both of us to get the information we need. It will give us an opportunity to ask questions about your background and experiences in order to make a fair evaluation of your application. It will also provide you with the opportunity to ask us for information that will help you decide whether or not the position meets your requirements."

3. Explain how the interview will be conducted.

Suggestion: "Initially we will ask you questions about your application documents. We will then ask a variety of planned questions related to our predetermined selection criteria. Toward the end of the interview we will describe the position and provide the answers to any questions you may have. Closing off the interview will be the last step of the interview."

4. Explain you will be taking notes throughout the interview.

Suggestion: "We will be taking notes throughout the interview. This will help us make a thorough and fair evaluation of your suitability for the position."

5. Explain the water and paper is for their use. Ask if there is anything more they need before starting.

Suggested transition comment: "I think we are ready to start. We will begin with some questions about your application materials."

APPENDIX

QUESTIONS ABOUT APPLICATION MATERIALS

Ask the questions you have noted from the review of the application materials and the initial screening interview. Remember to take notes of the candidate's answers.

\# 1. _____

_____

  Notes:

\# 2. _____

_____

  Notes:

\# 3. _____

_____

  Notes:

Acceptance Of Working Conditions: If not already done so in the screening interview, explain the important working conditions (hours of work, travel, overtime expectations, disciplining others etc.) and ask the candidate if they can accept them. If they cannot, you may want to end the interview at this point.

Previous Supervisors: If not already provided in the application materials, ask the candidate for the names and phone numbers of their previous Supervisors and ask for their permission to contact them. If they say no, be sure to ask why.

Name	Organization	Phone

Suggested Transition Comment: "Thanks for that information. Now we will ask you some questions pertaining to our selection criteria."

Behavioral Interviewing Guide

INITIATIVE: Willingly does work without being asked or waiting for instructions; self-starting; offers suggestions for improvement; voluntarily helps others; confronts and handles problems and situations.

Using your current/past job as a reference, provide two examples of doing more than what was expected of you.

Response: I –

              A –

              O –

Tell us about a time when you made a valuable work improvement suggestion?

Response: I –

              A –

              O –

Tell us about a time when you tackled a problem or situation that others avoided or refused to handle.

Response: I –

              A –

              O –

Back-up: Tell us about a time when you felt it necessary to change the way you did your job.

Response: I –

              A –

              O –

Oral Communication (+ or -): volume ( ) grammar ( ) vocabulary ( ) rate ( ) confident ( ) eye contact ( ) concise ( ) inflection/modulation ( ) initial impact ( ) holds attention ( )

Appendix

WORK STANDARDS: – Tasks are consistently completed in a thorough, accurate, timely and high quality manner; sets high standards for self and others; willingly spends extra time to make sure work is done well.

Give us two examples of when your work was more thorough, accurate or of better quality than your co-workers.

Response: I –

                     A –

                     O –

How many hours of overtime have you worked in the past three months?

Response: I –

                     A –

                     O –

Everyone at one time or another has had their work criticized or rejected. Tell us about a time when this happened to you.

Response: I –

                     A –

                     O –

Back-up: Tell us about a time when you went beyond the norm and put in extra hours to complete a task or project.

Response: I –

                     A –

                     O –

Oral Communication (+ or -): volume ( ) grammar ( ) vocabulary ( ) rate ( ) confident ( ) eye contact ( ) concise ( ) inflection/modulation ( ) initial impact ( ) holds attention ( )

BEHAVIORAL INTERVIEWING GUIDE

RELIABILITY: Can be counted on to meet performance expectations; completes assigned tasks and projects on time; does what they say they will do; reports to work on time; has a low level of absenteeism.

How many instances of absenteeism and lateness have you had in the last year and what were the reasons?

Response: I –

   A –

   O –

Periodically, everyone says they will do something for a co-worker and are unable to so for some reason. Describe a time when this has happened to you.

Response: I –

   A –

   O –

How did your last Supervisor evaluate your ability to meet his/her performance expectations?

Response: I –

   A –

   O –

Back-up: Describe a time when you were unable to complete a project or major task on time.

Response: I –

   A –

   O –

Oral Communication (+ or -): volume ( ) grammar ( ) vocabulary ( ) rate ( ) confident ( ) eye contact ( ) concise ( ) inflection/ modulation ( ) initial impact ( ) holds attention ( )

Appendix

HONESTY: Communicates with others in an honest and direct manner; does not distort, exaggerate or misrepresent information; does not show deceitful, manipulative, fraudulent, criminal or other unacceptable behavior; adheres to organizational policies and rules.

At times you have to bend a policy or rule to get the job done. Describe a time when you had to do this.

Response: I -

   A -

   O -

Tell us about a time when you were asked to compromise your principles or ethical standards.

Response: I -

   A -

   O -

Have you ever witnessed or been made aware of a fellow employee doing something inappropriate, unethical or illegal? Tell us about it.

Response: I -

   A -

   O -

Back-up: Have you every had to withhold information from your supervisor for what you felt was a justifiable reason. If so, tell us about the situation.

Response: I -

   A -

   O -

Oral Communication (+ or -): volume ( ) grammar ( ) vocabulary ( ) rate ( ) confident ( ) eye contact ( ) concise ( ) inflection/modulation ( ) initial impact ( ) holds attention ( )

ADAPTABILITY: Willingness and ability to adapt to changing conditions, processes, policies and laws; trying a different approach, option or solution when the current one is not working.

Tell us about a time when you really "dug in your heels" and refused to co-operate with a rule or policy change.

Response: I –

A –

O –

Give us an example of a time when things were not working and you seemed to have reached a dead end.

Response: I –

A –

O –

Describe some significant changes you have made in your personal life over the past two years.

Response: I –

A –

O –

Back-up: Tell us about a time when you felt it was better not to make a change when the opportunity presented itself.

Response: I –

A –

O –

Oral Communication (+ or -): volume ( ) grammar ( ) vocabulary ( ) rate ( ) confident ( ) eye contact ( ) concise ( ) inflection/modulation ( ) initial impact ( ) holds attention ( )

Appendix

PLANNING AND ORGANIZATION – Ability to identify and structure tasks/activities for self and others to complete an assignment or project.

How do you keep track of the tasks requiring your attention?

Response: I –

　　　　　 A –

　　　　　 O –

Have you ever been in a situation where you had too much to do and not enough time to do everything? Tell us about it.

Response: I –

　　　　　 A –

　　　　　 O –

Have you ever lead a project group or team? If so, tell us how you went about doing it.

Response: I –

　　　　　 A –

　　　　　 O –

Back-up: What types of planning and organizing do you do in your present job? What about previous jobs?

Response: I –

　　　　　 A –

　　　　　 O –

Oral Communication (+ or -): volume ( ) grammar ( ) vocabulary ( ) rate ( ) confident ( ) eye contact ( ) concise ( ) inflection/modulation ( ) initial impact ( ) holds attention ( )

BEHAVIORAL INTERVIEWING GUIDE

INTERPERSONAL SKILL: Ability to work harmoniously with others; skill at perceiving and reacting empathetically to the needs of others; treats people with consideration, sensitivity, kindness and fairness.

Tell us about a time in the last few days when you had to respond to a person empathetically.

Response: I –
               A –
               O –

Describe a time in the last year when you had a serious disagreement with a co-worker, boss or friend.

Response: I –
               A –
               O –

Have you ever had to give someone some news that impacted negatively on them? If so, please tell us about the situation.

Response: I –
               A –
               O –

Back-up: Give us a specific example of how you have built a relationship on trust and respect.

Response: I –
               A –
               O –

Oral Communication (+ or –): volume ( ) grammar ( ) vocabulary ( ) rate ( ) confident ( ) eye contact ( ) concise ( ) inflection/modulation ( ) initial impact ( ) holds attention ( )

Appendix

MENTAL ABILITY: Ability to identify, gather, analyze and understand information; to reach reasoned and sound conclusions, recommendations or decisions; to understand and assimilate new technology.

What was your grade point average in school and what courses were the easiest and the most difficult for you?

Response: I –

  A –

  O –

What has been the most difficult job related learning situation for you?

Response: I –

  A –

  O –

Everyone occasionally makes a bad decision. Describe a time when you made such a decision.

Response: I –

  A –

  O –

Back-up: Describe the most difficult problem you have had to deal with in the past year.

Response: I –

  A –

  O –

Oral Communication (+ or -): volume ( ) grammar ( ) vocabulary ( ) rate ( ) confident ( ) eye contact ( ) concise ( ) inflection/modulation ( ) initial impact ( ) holds attention ( )

DELEGATION SKILL: Ability to select and assign appropriate tasks to others; provide direction when necessary; establish and review completion dates.

Describe an important assignment you recently delegated to an employee.

Response: I –

 A –

 O –

Tell us about a time when you delegated a task to another person and it turned out badly.

Response: I –

 A –

 O –

In your job at _____ , what types of task or assignments would you not delegate to others? Please provide some examples.

Response: I –

 A –

 O –

Back-up: Describe a time when delegation worked as an effective development tool for you.

Response: I –

 A –

 O –

Oral Communication (+ or -): volume ( ) grammar ( ) vocabulary ( ) rate ( ) confident ( ) eye contact ( ) concise ( ) inflection/ modulation ( ) initial impact ( ) holds attention ( )

Appendix

CONTROL SKILL: Ability to establish appropriate control measures to monitor the results of their own work and the work of others; to stay on top of things and keep track.

In your current job, how do you keep track of what work has to be done?

Response: I –

A –

O –

How do you stay attuned to what your employees are doing on a day-to-day basis?

Response: I –

A –

O –

Describe a recent incident when the work went badly "off the rails."

Response: I –

A –

O –

Back-up: Most people, at one time or another, forget to follow-up on a task given to an employee. Describe a time when this has happened to you.

Response: I –

A –

O –

Oral Communication (+ or -): volume ( ) grammar ( ) vocabulary ( ) rate ( ) confident ( ) eye contact ( ) concise ( ) inflection/modulation ( ) initial impact ( ) holds attention ( )

LEADERSHIP ABILITY: Ability to coach, motivate or direct others to accomplish a task or achieve a goal; demonstrates leadership through personal example.

Describe a time when your leadership made the difference between success and failure.

Response: I –

A –

O –

Tell us about a time you were able to motivate your employees to accomplish a difficult objective.

Response: I –

A –

O –

Tell us about the toughest group you had to get co-operation from.

Response: I –

A –

O –

Back-up: What specific behaviors do you show to lead by example?

Response: I –

A –

O –

Oral Communication (+ or -): volume ( ) grammar ( ) vocabulary ( ) rate ( ) confident ( ) eye contact ( ) concise ( ) inflection/modulation ( ) initial impact ( ) holds attention ( )

Appendix

REQUIRED JOB KNOWLEDGE: The extent of the job related knowledge acquired and understood.

Critical Knowledge Area: _____

   Question:

   Answer:

Critical Knowledge Area: _____

   Question:

   Answer:

Critical Knowledge Area: _____

   Question:

   Answer:

Critical Knowledge Area: _____

   Question:

   Answer:

Critical Knowledge Area: _____

   Question:

   Answer:

Oral Communication (+ or -): volume ( ) grammar ( ) vocabulary ( ) rate ( ) confident ( ) eye contact ( ) concise ( ) inflection/ modulation ( ) initial impact ( ) holds attention ( )

Behavioral Interviewing Guide

_____ : _____
_____

?_____
_____

Response: I –
               A –
               O –

?_____
_____

Response: I –
               A –
               O –

?_____
_____

Response: I –
               A –
               O –

Back-up?_____
_____

Response: I –
               A –
               O –

Oral Communication (+ or -): volume ( ) grammar ( ) vocabulary ( ) rate ( ) confident ( ) eye contact ( ) concise ( ) inflection/ modulation ( ) initial impact ( ) holds attention ( )

Appendix

INTERVIEW CLOSE – SUGGESTED CONTENT

1. Explain to the candidate you are going to give them a question to think about and while they are doing their thinking you will look over your notes to ensure nothing has been left out.

   Suggested question – "Tell us about a time when you had to make a very unpopular decision."

2. Review your notes and note any areas in need of further questioning.

3. Ask the candidate for their response to the above question and note their answer.

   Response: I –

   A –

   O –

4. Ask any further questions you have noted and record the response(s).

5. If required, provide a description of the position.

6. Ask the candidate if they have any questions and, if so, note them below and answer them, if you can.

   Candidate's questions:

7. Explain the next step in the selection process and tell them when they can expect to hear the interview results.

8. Thank the candidate for the interview.

IMPORTANT: Begin the evaluation process immediately after the close. Do not start a second interview before completing this candidate's evaluation.

BEHAVIORAL INTERVIEWING GUIDE

CANDIDATE EVALUATION

Rate the candidate on each selection criterion. If a team format has been used it is very important that each interviewer independently rate the candidate first, and, afterwards, share those individual ratings with other team members and reach a consensus rating. Suggested rating scale:

5. A great deal of the criterion behavior was noted. **Excellent**
4. Quite a lot was described. **Good**
3. A satisfactory or average amount was noted. **Satisfactory**
2. Only a small amount was noted. **Less than satisfactory**
1. Little or no behavior was described in the interview. **Poor**

CRITERIA	INTERVIEWER RATINGS			CON-SENSUS	WEIGHT-ING	FINAL
	1	2	3			
Initiative						
Work Standards						
Reliability						
Honesty						
Adaptability						
Planning & Organization						
Interpersonal Skill						
Oral Communication						
Mental Ability						
Delegation Skill						
Control Skill						
Leadership Ability						
Job Knowledge						
	Overall Rating:					

APPENDIX

INTERVIEWERS:
_____, _____, _____

Areas To Follow-up On During The Background Check:

_____

_____

_____

APPENDIX B

CORE SELECTION CRITERIA

PERSONALITY ATTRIBUTES

- **INITIATIVE** – Willingly does work without being asked or waiting for instructions; self-starting; offers suggestions for improvement; voluntarily helps others; confronts and handles problems and situations.
- **WORK STANDARDS** – Work tasks are consistently completed in a thorough, accurate, timely and high quality manner; sets high standards for self and others; willingly spends extra time to make sure work is done well.
- **RELIABILITY** – Can be counted on to meet job performance expectations; completes assigned tasks and projects on time; does what they say they will do; reports to work on time; has a low level of absenteeism.
- **HONESTY** – Communicates with others in an honest and direct manner; does not distort, exaggerate or misrepresent information; does not show deceitful, manipulative, fraudulent, criminal or other unacceptable behavior; adheres to organizational policies and rules.
- **ADAPTABILITY** – Willingness and ability to adapt to changing conditions, processes, policies and laws; tries a different ap-

Appendix

proach, option or solution when the current one is not working.

ABILITIES AND SKILLS

- **PLANNING AND ORGANIZING** – Ability to identify and structure tasks/activities for self and others to complete an assignment or project.

- **INTERPERSONAL SKILL** – Ability to work harmoniously with others; skill at perceiving and reacting empathetically to the needs of others; treats people with consideration, sensitivity, kindness and fairness.

- **ORAL COMMUNICATION SKILL** – Ability to speak in a clear and concise manner that is easily understood by others; ability to listen to and understand the communication of others.

- **MENTAL ABILITY** – Ability to identify, gather, analyze and understand information; to reach reasoned and sound conclusions, recommendations or decisions; to understand and assimilate new technology.

- **DELEGATION SKILL*** - Ability to select and assign appropriate tasks to others; provide direction when necessary; establish and review completion dates.

- **CONTROL SKILL*** - Ability to establish appropriate control measures to monitor the results of their own work and the work of others; to stay on top of things and keep on track.

- **LEADERSHIP ABILITY*** – Ability to coach, motivate or direct others to accomplish a task or achieve a goal; demonstrates leadership through personal example.

*for management/supervisory positions

KNOWLEDGE

- **JOB SPECIFIC KNOWLEDGE** – The extent of job-specific knowledge learned and understood.

OTHER COMMON SELECTION CRITERIA

PERSONALITY ATTRIBUTES

- **TEAM ORIENTATION** – Willingness to work cooperatively with others as part of a team effort; demonstrates supportive and helpful behaviors towards fellow team members.
- **STRESS TOLERANCE** – Capacity to maintain good job performance and demonstrate stable behavior while under significant stress and pressure.
- **CUSTOMER ORIENTATION** – Ability to identify, understand and respond to needs of internal and external customers.

ABILITIES AND SKILLS

- **WRITING ABILITY** – Ability to express oneself clearly in writing in an organized and grammatical correct manner.
- **PHYSICAL ABILITY** – Ability to perform the required physical tasks inherent in the job; includes the dimensions of strength, dexterity, coordination, flexibility, endurance and visual acuity.

APPENDIX C

BEHAVIORAL QUESTIONS FOR CORE SELECTION CRITERIA

PERSONALITY ATTRIBUTES

INITIATIVE – Willingly does work without being asked or waiting for instructions; self-starting; offers suggestions for improvement; voluntarily helps others; confronts and handles problems and situations.

Tell us about a time when you made an improvement suggestion to your supervisor.

Describe how you prepared for this interview.

What personal skill development actions have you completed in the last year?

In your current job, how do you determine what tasks you will work on each day?

Describe a time when you tackled a tough and/or unpopular assignment.

In your current or previous job, describe two different times when you displayed exceptional or noteworthy initiative.

Have you ever received a formal award or commendation for taking initiative, either on the job or off? Tell us about it.

What community service are you currently involved with and tell us how you got involved and how much time you spend on it?

Using your current or previous job as a reference, describe the specific things you do to help your co-workers.

Using your current job as a reference point, describe two examples of you doing more than what is expected of you.

Tell us about a time when you tackled a problem or situation that others avoided or refused to handle.

Describe a project that was suggested, planned and implemented mainly through your efforts.

Tell us about a time when you felt it necessary to change the way you do your job.

Tell us about any additional training or education you have completed since graduating from high school, college or university.

Have you ever been confronted by a problem situation that you felt your boss should handle but they were not there to do so? Tell us about it.

In your current position, how do you assist others to do their job?

How have your responsibilities changed since you started your current job?

What goals have you set and achieved in the last two years?

Give us an example of a time you worked the hardest and felt the greatest sense of achievement.

How was your college, university or vocational education financed?

Tell us what you know about this organization.

Tell us about a time when you had to defend an idea or decision to your boss.

APPENDIX

WORK STANDARDS – Work tasks are completed thoroughly, accurately, in a timely manner and with good quality; sets high standards for self and others; willingly puts in the time, however long it takes, to do the job.

On your current job, how do you personally assess how well you are performing?

✓ Give us two examples of when your work was more thorough, accurate or of a higher quality than you co-workers.

Describe a time when you and your supervisor had a disagreement about your work performance.

Tell us about a time when you had to make a formal presentation of at least one hour or more.

✓ Tell us about a time when you had more work than you could reasonably handle in a normal workday.

Have you ever completed and printed off a lengthy report ready for submission only to discover some minor errors? Describe the circumstances.

Describe a time when your work demands conflicted with your family needs.

Have you ever received recognition for exceptional work? Tell us about it.

Give us two examples where people came to you to do additional work because you had done a good job for them before.

Describe a time when your work was not up to your personal standards.

✓ Everyone at some time has had their work criticized or rejected. Tell us about a time when this has happened to you.

Have you ever had to discipline or fire an employee for poor work performance? Please describe the circumstances.

Tell us about a time when you went beyond the norm and put in extra hours to complete a task.

Behavioral Interviewing Guide

Describe a time when a problem was not resolved to your satisfaction.

Did your grades in school represent your best achievement? Please comment.

In your current job, how do you value or measure the success of your work?

How many hours of overtime have you voluntarily worked in the last three months?

Tell us about a time when you delivered more work than was expected.

Have you ever been in a situation when you had to disregard the instructions of your Supervisor? Tell us about the situation.

Have you ever been in a job situation when you felt you were being stuck with all the work? Please explain the circumstances.

Tell us about a few of your achievements that have been recognized by your supervisors.

What were some of your most important accomplishments in your job at _____ ?

What areas of your work have been criticized most often?

Tell us about some task or project you started but could not finish.

Describe a time when you were criticized for the way you handled a project.

How did your last supervisor evaluate your performance?

RELIABILITY – Can be counted on to meet job performance expectations; completes assigned tasks and projects on time; does what they say they will do; reports to work on time; has a low level of absenteeism.

How many absenteeism days did you have in the last two years and what were the reasons?

Appendix

How many days have you been late for work in the last year and what were the reasons?

How did your last supervisor rate your reliability with regards to doing your work, attendance, reporting to work on time and leaving work on time?

Describe two times in the last year when you told someone you would do something and you worked through adversity to do it.

Periodically, everyone has promised to do something for a co-worker or supervisor and for whatever reason, they were unable to follow through on that promise. Tell us about a time when this has happened to you.

Describe a time when you were unable to complete a project or major task on time.

Tell us about a task or project you started, but had to abandon.

At one time or another, everyone has been told their work did not meet the organization's expectations. Tell us about a time when this happened to you.

How often have you missed deadlines in the last two years.

Describe a time when a close friend or colleague said you let them down.

Have you ever cancelled an important family event in order to work late or come in on your day off? Please explain the circumstances.

HONESTY – Communicates with others in an honest and direct manner; does not distort, exaggerate or misrepresent information; does not show deceitful, manipulative, fraudulent, criminal or other unacceptable behavior; adheres to organizational policies and rules.

Have you ever been convicted of a criminal offence related to the position under consideration?

Have you ever been refused bonding? If so, please explain the circumstances.

At work, we have all had to avoid telling the truth at one time or another. Tell us about a time you had to do this and the circumstances that required it.

In your opinion, what percentage of employees steal items such as stationary, tools, materials and equipment from their employer?

In your opinion, what percentage of employees inflate or "pad" their expense accounts?

Describe a time when you had to communicate some very negative, potentially hurtful information to another person.

Tell us about a time when you had to provide performance feedback to a poor performer.

Have you ever been fired from a job? If so, tell us about the circumstances.

Describe a time when you had to say no to a colleague or employee and you felt very uncomfortable for having done so.

Tell us about a time when you were asked to compromise your principles or ethical standards.

When was the last time you had to admit you were wrong? Please explain the circumstances.

Have you ever been in a situation where people questioned your honesty or integrity? Please tell us about it.

Describe a recent moral or ethical dilemma you have encountered.

Everyone has to bend the rules some time in order to get the job done. Describe a time when you had to do this.

Tell us about a time when you were unable to meet a commitment that you made.

Everyone has had to withhold information from a direct report, supervisor, fellow employee or customer for a justifiable reason. Tell us about a time when you had to do this.

Describe a time when you had to bend your personal standards to get the job done.

Appendix

Have you ever been counselled or disciplined for breaking a company rule or policy? If so, tell us about the situation.

When attending school, did you ever encounter a person paying to get a paper, essay of thesis written for them? Please tell us about the incident.

Tell us about your experience with working in a position of trust.

Have you ever been asked to do something you considered immoral or unethical? Please describe the situation.

Have you ever witnessed or been made aware of a fellow employee doing something inappropriate, unethical or immoral? Tell us about it.

Have you ever been in a situation when a customer wanted a more expensive product or service but you knew they only needed a less expensive one? If so, please describe the situation.

ADAPTABILITY – Willingness and ability to adapt to changing conditions, processes, policies and laws; tries a different approach, option or solution when the current one is not working.

Describe a job related circumstance when you had to make a significant change in the way you had been doing things.

Tell us about a time when you felt it was better not to change your approach when the opportunity to change presented itself.

Have you ever been in a situation when you disagreed with a new organizational policy or rule? Tell us about it.

Describe some significant changes you have made in your personal life over the past two years.

In the last year, how have you changed the way you do your job?

Tell us about a time when you really "dug in your heels" and refused to co-operate with a rule or policy change.

Give us an example of a time when things were not working and you seemed to have reached a dead end.

Have you ever had a person express the sentiment of, "why change when the way we are doing it is working?" If so, tell us about the situation.

Tell us about a time when you were asked to do some work outside the normal scope of your job.

Tell us about a time when you made a successful adaptation to a change in process, policy or condition.

Explain to us, the extent of your computer knowledge and skills.

Describe the types of job training you have completed in the last two or three years.

Tell us about a time when you had trouble selling your supervisor on an idea.

Tell us about a time when there was no set procedure or precedent to help you solve a problem.

What setbacks or failures have you had in your life?

Tell us about a time you had to overcome a big obstacle to get the task or project done.

What crisis situations have you been confronted with in the last year?

Describe a time when your supervisors rejected a recommendation you had made.

Describe a time when you became aware of new technology that could help your organization and you went ahead and applied it.

Tell us about a time when you seemed to be on the wrong side of an issue.

ABILITIES AND SKILLS CRITERIA

PLANNING AND ORGANIZING – Ability to identify and structure tasks/activities for self and others to complete an assignment or project.

Appendix

Describe what you do when you go into work on a normal workday.

Have you ever been in a situation where you had too much to do and not enough time to do everything? Tell us about it.

Have you ever lead a project group or team? Tell us about it.

Tell us about a time when you had to extend a deadline.

Describe a time when a project you were working on turned out badly.

Have you ever had to schedule a lot of work for a number of people? If so, please tell us about the situation.

Please describe the types of planning and organizing experiences you had in your last or current job(s). Please be specific in explaining the types of planning done.

What were your career goals on leaving school?

Give us an example of how you prioritize a list of tasks or assignments.

Do you handle your personal affairs like bill payment, insurances, wills, household matters, car maintenance, banking, pension plans etc.? If so, how do you go about doing this?

Did you prepare a personal budget last year? If so, how did you do it?

Do you have plans for your retirement? Please tell us about them.

What types of planning and organizing do you do in your present job?

How do you keep track of the things requiring your attention?

Tell us about one of your projects that was not completed.

How do you plan and organize a major project? Give us a specific example.

At one time or another everyone has something "fall through the cracks." Describe a time when this happened to you.

Tell us about the problems you face in getting all your work done.

Describe a time when you found yourself overloaded with work.

Describe some time saving ideas you have incorporated into your behavior.

Tell us about a time when an unexpected project was assigned to you.

INTERPERSONAL SKILL – Ability to work harmoniously with others; skill at perceiving and reacting empathetically to the needs of others; treats people with consideration, sensitivity, kindness and fairness.

Describe a time in the last six months when you had a conflict or serious disagreement with a fellow employee.

Tell us about a time in the last few days when you had to respond to another person in an empathetic fashion.

Describe two or three behaviors you have shown in the last month that have resulted in an improved relationship with a co-worker.

At one time or another everyone has a co-worker accuse you of being unfair, insensitive or unkind. Tell us about a time when this has happened to you.

How many close friends do you have?

When have you provided a fellow employee the opportunity to "save face?" Please provide a specific example.

Have you ever left a situation knowing you hurt someone's feelings? Please tell us about it.

Tell us about a time when you had to support someone going through a difficult time in their life.

Have you ever had to give someone some news that had a strong negative impact on them? Please tell us about the circumstances.

Tell us about a time when you saved someone from embarrassment.

Appendix

Tell us about a time when you were not fully accepted by your co-workers.

Have you ever been wrongly criticized? If so, please tell us about the circumstances.

Have you ever worked with an overly critical person? If so, please explain the circumstances.

Tell us about a time in the last six months when a person has asked for your assistance or advice on how they should handle a work or personal problem?

⇒ What specific behaviors do you consistently use to show respect for others?

How do you go about building a trusting and respectful relationship? Give us a specific example of when you have done this.

Please provide us with three examples of using positive recognition in the last two weeks.

Have you ever worked with a team of employees where one member was not pulling their weight? If so, explain the situation and circumstances.

⇒ Tell me about a time when you had to customize or tailor your communication to fit the background or experiences of your listener.

Have you ever worked with a person who consistently wasted your time? Tell us about it.

Tell me about a time when you regretted your comments or behavior in a work place situation.

When have your diplomacy skills been put to the test? Tell us about it.

How have you enhanced the self-esteem of the people you work with?

Have you ever worked with a person you really disliked? If so, describe the situation for us.

BEHAVIORAL INTERVIEWING GUIDE

Has you behaviour ever caused another person a problem? Tell us about the situation and circumstances.

How did you handle an arrogant, know-it-all type of person that you had to get along with?

When was the last time you had a personality clash with a co-worker?

Tell us about a difficult interpersonal work situation that you have been involved in.

Describe a time when humor played a part on how you handled a situation or person.

Tell us about a time when you had to handle a frustrated and angry internal or external customer.

Have you ever had a person lose their temper with you? Tell us about it.

How did you go about establishing a relationship with your previous supervisor?

Using previous work experiences as a reference point, describe the type of people you work well with and those you don't.

Have you ever been involved in a downsizing situation? Tell us about your co-workers who lost their jobs.

Have you ever had to introduce a new system, process, method or technology? Explain how you did it.

ORAL COMMUNICATION SKILL – Ability to speak in a clear and concise manner that is easily understood by others; ability to listen to and understand the communication of others.

Note: A person's oral communication skill can be assessed during the interview by carefully observing and recording their speaking and listening behavior. The areas to assess are as follows: for speaking - clarity, volume, vocabulary, organization, inflection/modulation, persuasiveness, grammar and syntax; for listening - number of times the interviewee asks the interviewer to repeat the question, whether or not eye contact is made, whether or not

Appendix

the interviewee interrupts the interviewer and whether or not the interviewee's responses indicate understanding of the questions.

Have you ever had to convince a person to do something when they were initially very resistant about doing it? If so, tell us about it.

Tell us about a time when you communicated badly.

Do people frequently ask you to repeat your oral communications? Give me some specific examples when this has happened.

Tell us about a time when you told someone to do something and they did it wrong.

What are some of the most difficult or complex pieces of information you have had to communicate.

Describe a time when you had to customize or tailor your communication to fit the background or experiences of your listener.

How do you show others that you are listening to them? Provide a specific example please.

Give us some examples from your present job where you get important information verbally.

How often do you present information to groups? Tell us about the circumstances.

Everyone at one time or another has been uncomfortable in a communication situation. Describe a time when this has happened to you.

All of us, at one time or another, have had difficulty explaining something over the phone. Give us an example when this has happened to you.

Tell us about a time when you had to persuade others to adopt your idea.

Tell us about a time when you listened poorly.

How do you react to a person who rambles and talks to excess? Give us a recent job example.

We all have times when we misinterpret information. Tell us about a time when this has happened to you.

Give us an example where your listening changed your course of action on handling a situation?

Have you ever had to separate yourself emotionally from a listening situation? Tell us about it.

Has anyone ever told you to stop interrupting? Please explain the circumstances.

Tell us what empathetic listening means and give us an example when you used the skill.

What difficulties have you encountered communicating with others?

Asking questions about oral communication is not as effective as observing it in the interview or using a **simulation exercise of a job related communication situation**. *For example, if the job requires the incumbent to communicate policy information to others, then prepare a simulation exercise where you ask the interviewee to read written descriptive information on a policy change and then ask them to prepare and verbally communicate the information to an employee/ role player (interviewer).*

MENTAL ABILITY – Ability to identify, gather, analyze and understand information; to reach reasoned and sound conclusions, recommendations or decisions; to understand and assimilate new technology.

What was your grade point average in school?

What school courses were your easiest and which ones most difficult?

What has been the most difficult job related learning situation you have experienced?

How long did it take for you to feel comfortable in your job at _____?

Describe a situation where you have had to make a critical decision based on a small amount of information.

Appendix

Tell us about a decision that could have had serious consequences had you been wrong.

At one time or another, everyone makes a bad decision, describe a time when you felt you made such a decision.

Describe a situation when you had to determine whether to handle the situation yourself or call in someone else with more expertise.

Describe the most difficult problem you have had to deal with in the last year.

In your job at _____ , what decisions were the most difficult for you?

Give us an example when you had to overcome an obstacle or problem in an innovative way.

Tell us about a time when you had to learn something difficult in a short period of time.

What is the quickest and easiest way for you to learn new things? Provide a specific example please.

What techniques do you use to assimilate a lot of information in a short period of time? Please give us a specific example of when you had to use these techniques.

Describe a time when you concluded the risks outweighed the rewards.

Have you ever resolved a long-standing problem? Tell us about it.

What big problems did you encounter in your last job? Tell us about them.

Tell us about a time when you were confronted by a problem that should have been handled by your supervisor but they were not there to do so.

How do you decide when to ask for advice? Give us a specific example.

How many training courses have you attended over the last three years?

Describe a time when you learned a new technology and then applied it to your work.

Describe a very unpopular decision you had to make.

Tell us about a problem situation that you handled in a unique or innovative way.

Tell us about a time you made an important decision after seeking input from other employees.

Have you ever applied a solution that you used in a previous work situation to a problem in a different organization? Tell us about it.

How much initial training and coaching did you receive in your last job?

DELEGATION SKILL – Ability to select and assign appropriate tasks to others; provide direction when necessary; establish review and completion dates.

Describe an important assignment you recently delegated to an employee.

Tell us about a time when you delegated a tasks to another person and it turned out badly.

In your job at _____ , what types of tasks or assignments did you not delegate to others? Please provide some examples.

Describe a time when delegation worked as an effective management tool for you.

Describe a time when you delegated a task that really needed your attention but you did not have the time to spend on it.

Do you assign work to others? If so, describe how you go about it.

Tell us about a time when you decided not to delegate and it turned out to be a mistake.

Tell us about a time when you used delegation as an employee development tool.

How do you follow-up on delegated tasks after you have been away from work for some time?

Appendix

CONTROL SKILL - Ability to establish appropriate control measures to monitor the results of their own work and the work of others; to stay on top of things and keep on track.

What control methods do you use in your job at _____ ?

How do you stay attuned to what is going on with your direct reports?

How do you measure the performance of your employees?

Describe a recent incident where the work went "off the rails."

How do you keep track of what work you need to accomplish? Give us a specific example.

Do you use an electronic calendar/scheduler? How do you use it?

Have you ever lead a project team? How did you ensure that tasks were being done and progress was being made? Please provide a specific example.

At one time or another, every supervisor forgets to follow-up on something they delegated to another person. Describe a time when this has happened to you?

What control measures do you use to monitor the work of your employees?

How do you keep track of what your employees are doing.

What specific control indices do you use to monitor performance in your work unit.

LEADERSHIP ABILITY – Ability to coach, motivate or direct others to accomplish a task or achieve a goal; demonstrates leadership through personal example.

Describe a time when your leadership made the difference between success and failure.

Tell us about a time you were able to motivate your staff to accomplish a difficult objective.

Have you ever disciplined an employee? Tell us about it.

BEHAVIORAL INTERVIEWING GUIDE

What behaviors do you show in order to lead by example? Please provide specific examples.

Describe a time when careful and persistent coaching allowed an employee of yours to perform well.

Have you ever knowingly withheld information from your employees? Tell us about it.

What is the absenteeism rate of your employees?

Have you ever had to lead a group of people over whom you had no direct authority? Tell us about it.

Describe a time when you successfully coached a co-worker.

Tell us about a time when a colleague asked you for advice or direction.

Have you ever been in an "informal" leadership position? Tell us about it.

Describe a time when you felt you let a co-worker down.

Do your friends ask you for advice? Tell us about a time they have done so.

Have you ever been voted into a leadership position by colleagues or friends? Tell us about the circumstances.

Describe a time when you acted on someone's work improvement idea.

Tell us about a time when you had to make an unpopular decision.

Have you ever been in a situation when employees were not accepting your ideas? Please tell us about the circumstances.

Tell us about the toughest group you had to get cooperation from.

Tell us about a time when you took someone "under your wing."

Describe a time when you determined someone needed coaching when others had not picked up on it.

Have you ever had to train a new employee? If so, tell us how you went about it.

Appendix

Tell us about the objectives you have for your current work group.

Tell us about your current workplace diversity efforts.

Have you ever had to withhold information from an employee? Tell us about it.

Tell us about a person who was promoted as a result of your coaching efforts.

Who takes over your job duties when you are away?

Tell us about a time when you recognized a skill deficiency in an employee when others had missed it.

Give us some examples of when you have trained your employees to assume more responsibility.

KNOWLEDGE CRITERIA

JOB SPECIFIC KNOWLEDGE - The extent of job specific knowledge learned and understood.

Describe the various areas of your technical expertise.

We notice you have worked with (insert job specific knowledge area). What have you found to be its strengths and weaknesses?

What practical experience have you had with (insert job specific knowledge area)?

Tell us how you stay current in (insert job specific knowledge area).

Please note: To be able to use the following question formats you have to first identify and define the important job specific knowledge areas required for the position under consideration. These knowledge areas are then inserted into the appropriate question formats. We will use the job of a Management Trainer as an example. Some of the specific and critical knowledge areas needed for this position are as follows:

Adult learning principles.

Learning methods.

Preparing instructional objectives.

Preparing a power point presentation.

Handling difficult classroom situations.

Oral presentation techniques.

Management practices.

The bracketed parts of the following questions pertain to the specific knowledge areas listed above.

When you designed (your last training program, what adult learning principles did you design into the format)?

What is an (in-basket exercise and where can it be used effectively)?

Verbally, provide us with (an instructional objective for teaching managers the delegation skill)?

Explain how to (demote text when preparing a power point presentation)?

Is this statement true or false? (When you are making a formal oral presentation you should stand still and not move around the room).

What procedure do you follow to (handle a class participant who is overly critical of other participants)?

How do you (effectively cue a training video)?

How do you use the following (learning methods – role playing, programmed instruction and tests)?

Name three ways (you can advance to the next slide in a power point presentation)?

Which of the following is not a visual aid? (flip chart, overhead projector, white board, simulation).

Job knowledge can be effectively assessed using a **pencil and paper job knowledge test that is specifically prepared for this purpose**. The written test can be administered before or after the interview, individually or as a group.

Appendix

OTHER COMMON SELECTION CRITERIA

PERSONALITY ATTRIBUTES

TEAM ORIENTATION – Willingness to work cooperatively with others as part of a team effort; demonstrates supportive and helpful behaviors towards fellow team members.

In your previous positions, did you work independently or were you part of a team effort? If you worked as part of a team, how did you contribute.

Describe a time when you abandoned your personal needs or objectives in order to help the team.

Have you ever been part of a work team that did not work well? If so, tell us about it.

Tell us about a time you lead an effective team effort.

What off-job team activities are you involved with?

Have you ever been part of a work group when one or two of the members were not pulling their weight? Tell us about it.

What specific behaviors do you show to promote better team spirit?

At one time or other, everyone finds themselves in a team that is working poorly. Please tell us when this has happened to you.

STRESS TOLERANCE – Capacity to maintain good job performance and demonstrate stable behaviour while under significant stress and pressure.

Tell us about the most stressful situation you have encountered in the last six months.

Describe a time when your behavior was impacted by a stressful situation.

In your last position, what were your most significant stressors.

What has been the most uncomfortable interpersonal situation you have experienced in the last few years'.

What stress management techniques have you used frequently.

Tell us about the last time you really got angry about a management decision.

Tell us about the last time you lost your temper.

Have you ever been under the influence of tranquilizers or other mood altering drugs at work?

How do you relax? Please provide specific examples.

In the last year, when have you been the most upset with yourself? Please describe the situation.

At one time or another, everyone feels they may not have performed well under pressure. Describe a time when you felt like this?

Has a co-worker caused you to become irritated and frustrated? Tell us about the situation.

Have you ever felt burned out in a job? If so, please explain the circumstances.

CUSTOMER ORIENTATION – Capacity to identify and respond appropriately to the needs of either internal or external customers; understands the importance of good customer relations.

Tell us about your typical customer contact situations in your last job.

Describe a time when you had to go the extra mile to support an internal/external customer.

Have you ever identified a customer need before others? If so, tell us about it.

Have you ever given your home telephone number to a customer? If so, describe the circumstances.

What has been the most serious customer complaint situation you have had to handle?

What difficulties have you had handling customer relation situations?

Appendix

What types of customers make you mad and upset? Provide some specific examples.

Describe a time when you "salvaged" a customer that appeared lost.

What type of formal training have you had in customer relations.

When was the last time you lost your temper with an internal or external customer? Tell us about the circumstances.

Have you ever received a customer service award? Tell us about it?

How do you know you are giving the customer what they want? Provide a specific example.

ABILITIES AND SKILLS

WRITING ABILITY – Ability to express oneself clearly in writing in an organized and grammatical correct manner.

What types or written documents do you prepare in your current job? What about your previous job(s)?

How does your Email message writing differ from the writing you do in other aspects of your current job?

Have you ever received awards or recognition for your writing? Tell us about them.

What were your English grammar and composition marks like in school?

How did your previous supervisors evaluate your writing skills?

Using your current or previous job as a reference point, describe how you prepared a lengthy narrative report.

Have you ever published any articles or books? If so, tell us what they were.

The selection interview is not a good method for assessing writing ability. Obtaining an actual sample of the candidate's writing is a better method. Before or after the interview, ask the candidate to write a one or two page explanation of how he/she thinks they are qualified for the position under consideration. Evaluate the writing for legibility, grammar, spelling, organization, vocabulary and persuasiveness.

PHYSICAL ABILITY – Ability to perform the required physical tasks inherent in the job. Includes the dimensions of strength, muscle endurance, manual dexterity, eye/hand coordination, flexibility, cardio vascular endurance and visual acuity.

We are going to ask you about the physical requirements of the job. Are you able to (describe the physical requirements and obtain the candidate's responses).

Have you have any physical limitations or accommodation needs with respect to the position under consideration? If so, please explain.

Do you have any job related limitations or accommodation needs with respect to your strength, manual dexterity, eye/hand coordination, flexibility, muscle and vascular endurance and visual acuity? Any phobias and allergies related to the job under consideration?

The best way to assess the physical capability of a candidate is to design and implement a physical testing process that each candidate must successfully complete. Such a process would include a representative sample of all the actual physical tasks to be performed in the job. Examples: Continuously lift 50lb bags, climb stairs, stand for long periods of time, bend over repeatedly, push and pull heavy objects, work in a hot atmosphere for an hour without a rest break, crawling into confined spaces etc.

APPENDIX D

EXAMPLE CANDIDATE RATING SUMMARY SHEET

Rate the candidate on each selection criterion. If a team/panel format has been used it is very important to have each interviewer independently rate the candidate first and then share their individual ratings with each other and subsequently reach a consensus. The following rating scale is suggested:

5. A great deal of the criterion was described. **Excellent**
4. Quite a lot was described. **Good**
3. A satisfactory or average amount was described. **Satisfactory**
2. Only a small amount was described. **Less than satisfactory**
1. Little or no behavior was described in the interview. **Poor**

CRITERIA	INTERVIEWER RATINGS			CON-SENSUS	WEIGHT-ING	FINAL
	1	2	3			
Initiative	3	3	3	3	3	9
Work Standards	3	4	4	4	3	12
Reliability	4	4	4	4	3	12
Honesty	3.5	4	4	4	2	8
Adaptability	2.5	3	2.75	2.5	1	2.5
Planning & Organization	4	4	3	4	2	8
Interpersonal Skill	3	3	3	3	2	6
Oral Communication	5	4	4	4	1	4
Mental Ability	4	4	3.5	4	2	8
	Overall Rating: 69.5 out of 95 = 73.16% or 3.66 out of 5					

APPENDIX E

BACKGROUND CHECKING GUIDE FOR CORE SELECTION CRITERIA (TELEPHONE)

Date: _____ Time: _____ Interviewer: _____

Candidates Name: _____

Person Contacted: _____ Phone: _____

Position Of Contact: _____

Relationship Of Contact To Candidate: _____

1. Introduce yourself and explain the purpose of your call.

   "Hello Mr./Ms. _(Referee)_ , my name is _____ of _____ . Mr./Ms. __(Candidate)____ has applied for the position of _____ with our organization. Mr./Ms. _____ has told us you were their supervisor and has authorized us to speak with you. I would like to ask you about his/her on job behavior. It will take about 15 minutes. Is this a good time for you or would you prefer I call back at a more convenient time?"

2. If applicable, advise the person that it may be necessary to disclose their reference information and make it available to the candidate if it is requested pursuant to Federal, State/Provincial laws.

3. Confirm factual information provided by candidate – position held, length of service, dates of employment, reason for leaving,

APPENDIX

    major responsibilities/accountabilities, relationship to candidate etc.

4. Ask the following questions and record the responses.

    Please comment on their initiative and willingness to do work without being asked or waiting for instructions. (initiative)

    Please comment on the quality and quantity of their work. (work standards)

    Were they reliable with respect to meeting performance expectations, completing assignments, reporting to work on time and adhering to break times? (reliability)

    Are they honest and direct with others? Are they ethical? Do they follow rules and policies? (honesty)

    Comment on their willingness to adapt to changing conditions, processes and policies. (adaptability)

    Are they well organized and do they plan their work and the work of others effectively? (planning and organizing)

    Are they good at working with others and do they treat their fellow employees with consideration and kindness? (interpersonal skill)

    How would you describe their speaking and listening skills? (oral communication)

    Please comment on their thinking ability. How quickly did they learn new tasks? (mental ability)

    Please comment on their delegation skill. Were they effective at assigning work to others? (delegation skill)

    Did they make use of effective controls to monitor the work of others? (control skill)

Behavioral Interviewing Guide

Please comment on their ability to direct, coach, motivate and inspire their employees. Were they a good role model? (leadership)

How would you describe the extent of their job related knowledge in the following areas of importance? (job specific knowledge)

_____

_____

_____

?(other criteria)_____
_____
? _____
_____

5. Ask the following general questions.

    Were there any performance areas that you would have liked to have seen them do better at?

    Were there any personal problems that negatively impacted their work that I should know about, such as addictions, medical conditions and personality disorders?

    Please comment on their personal grooming and hygiene.

    Would you re-hire this person? (If they respond "no" be sure to ask why.)

    Is there any other job related information you would like to provide that you think would be important for me to know?

6. Close of the interview.

    "Thank you very much for your information and I can assure you it will be treated discreetly and confidently."

7. Evaluate the background check.

Appendix

- ❏ Information obtained would indicate no problems and corroborates the interview information and ratings.
- ❏ Information is vague, generalized, inconsistent or inconclusive. More referees need to be contacted.
- ❏ Information indicates definite problems with certain selection criteria.
- ❏ Contact would not provide any information about the selection criteria.

Recommendation: _____

BEHAVIORAL INTERVIEWING MATERIALS AND SERVICES

The following materials and services are available on request. Please contact us for current prices.

Materials:

- Additional copies of the Behavioral Interviewing Guide
- Interview Selection Guides for management/supervisory positions.
- Interview Selection Guides for non-management positions.
- Background Check Guides for management/supervisory positions.
- Background Check Guides for non-management positions.

Services: (Contact us for a fee quote.)

- Determining job specific selection criteria.
- Determining job specific behavioral questions.
- Preparing job specific Interview Guides.
- Preparing job specific Background Check Guides.
- Preparing of customized copies of the Behavioral Interviewing Guide.

Phone – 604 . 532 . 5947

Email – sales@intelligentselection.net

Web Address – www.intelligentselection.net

Mailing Address – Intelligent Selection Inc.

2690 224th St.

Langley, B.C. Canada V2Z 3B3

ISBN 1-41204285-2